The Pan-Celtic Phrasebook

le recueil d'expressions pan-celtiques

WELSH · IRISH · GAELIC · BRETON
gallois · irlandais · gaélique · breton

First impression: 1998
Second impression: 1999
Première édition: 1998
Deuxième édition: 1999

© Y Lolfa Cyf. & William Knox, 1998

Illustrations/*Dessins:* Elwyn Ioan

Printed and published in Wales by
Imprimé et edité au Pays de Galles par
Y Lolfa Cyf., Talybont, Ceredigion SY24 5AP
✉ylolfa@ylolfa.com 🖳www.ylolfa.com
☎+ 44 (0)1970 832 304 🖹832 782 isdn832 813

The Pan-Celtic Phrasebook

le recueil d'expressions pan-celtiques

William Knox

y Lolfa

The Celtic Countries Les Pays Celtiques

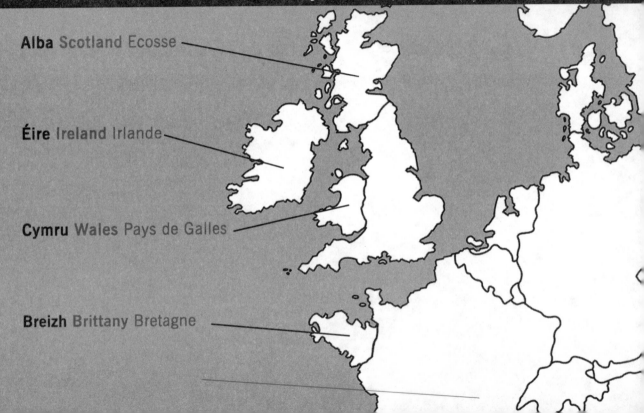

Alba Scotland Ecosse

Éire Ireland Irlande

Cymru Wales Pays de Galles

Breizh Brittany Bretagne

No lessons.
No grammar.
Not even an index!

Pas de leçons
ni de grammaire.
Même pas d'indexe!

Something <u>underlined</u> like <u>*the car*</u> in one phrase is the equivalent of what is <u>underlined</u> in the other phrases. The <u>underlines</u> do not denote emphasis. If you want to know a specific word, search the appropriate heading. An "=" shows a variant of a word or helps explain something.

There are no YES or NO in the Celtic languages. In general, you answer the verb with the same verb (describer) and the copula (identifier) with the same copula. Celtic consonant mutations are shown in bold. The word **dydd** for example has mutated to **ddydd**. After the phrase you will see **d**>**dd**, showing that the **d** mutates to **dd**.

Les mots <u>soulignés</u> sont des équivalents des mots <u>soulignés</u> dans les autres expressions. Les <u>soulignes</u> ne dénotent pas d'insistance. Si vous cherchez un mot, cherchez la rubrique la plus vraisemblable. Le "=" explique une variante d'un mot ou d'une autre chose.

Il n'y a ni de OUI ni de NON dans les langues celtiques. Généralement, on répond avec le verbe (pour décrire) dans la question avec le même verbe, et la copule (pour identifier) avec la même copule. Les mutations consonantiques des langues celtiques sont mises en caractères gras. Le mot **dydd** par exemple a changé en **dd**ydd. Après l'expression vous voyez **d**>**dd**, qui démonstre que le **d** change en **dd**.

Contents

pronounciation and mutation	9
greetings	25
apologies	37
travelling	41
in the car	49
bus and train	57
sports	63
illness	67
emergencies	71
shopping	75
the weather	79
signs	83
place names	91
food	95
drink	105
in the hotel	111
on the town	119
money	131
exploring	135
culture and entertainment	139
some proverbs	147
numbers	151
time	157
to be	165
possession	175
information and addresses	185
the media	195

la prononciation et les mutations	9	boissons	105
saluer	25	à l'hôtel	111
regrets	37	en ville	119
voyager	41	argent	131
en voiture	49	à la découverte	135
bus et train	57	culture et divertissement	139
sport	63	des proverbes	147
maladie	67	numéros	151
urgences	71	le temps	157
les courses	75	être	165
le temps	79	posséder	175
la signalisation	83	informations et adresses	185
noms de lieux	91	le média	195
alimentation	95		

pronounciation and mutation
ynganu a'r treigladau
an fuaimniú agus an múthú
am fuaimneachadh agus am muthadh
an distagadur hag ar c'hemmadurioù
la prononciation et les mutations

Pronouncing Irish

There are three types of consonant mutation:

1. **PALATALIZATION**=putting a narrow vowel I,E beside the consonant(s).
   or
   BROADENING=putting a broad vowel A,O,U beside the consonant(s).

2. **LENITION**=adding an H after it; like changing D to DH.

3. **ECLIPSIS**=covering the consonant with another; like changing D to ND.

Sometimes you will see a consonant or consonant cluster which has been dropped in speech.

It doesn't matter which side of the consonant the narrow or broad vowel touches; it affects the consonant or consonant cluster. If there are vowels on both sides of a consonant or consonant cluster, they both must be broad, or both be slender. For example, the *n* in *dún* (a fort) is not the same as the *n* in *dúin* (of a fort), and notice that in the word *duine* (a person), it is a narrow vowel which comes after the *n*, since it is a narrow vowel which precedes it.

There are other mutations which happen, for example, S changing to tS and a vowel having an N or H or T put in front of it. These "mutations" do not go under the above categories.

Vowels are vaguely like in Latin, but can become unclear if not on the first syllable. It is on the first syllable that the stress is put in most dialects. Diphthongs present a problem at first, as they make quite different sounds, however even these follow a pattern.

Il y a trois types de mutation consonantique:

1. **PALATISER**=mettre une voyelle frontale I,E à la consonne.

   ou

   DÉPALATISER=mettre une voyelle postérieure A,O,U à la consonne.

2. **LÉNIFIER**=mettre un H après; comme changer D en DH.

3. **ÉCLIPSER**=éclipser la consonne avec une autre; comme changer D en ND.

On voit quelque fois une consonne ou un groupe de consonnes qui s'avale.

Peu importe quel côté la voyelle frontale ou la voyelle postérieure touche; elle affectue la consonne ou le groupe de consonnes. S'il y a des voyelles sur les deux côtés de la consonne ou du groupe de consonnes, il faut que les deux soient postérieures ou qu'elles soient frontales. Par exemple, le *n* en *dún* (une fortresse) n'est pas le même *n* qu'en *dúin* (d'une fortresse [au génetif]). Voyez aussi que dans le mot *duine* (un homme), c'est une voyelle frontale qui suit le *n*, parce que c'est une voyelle frontale qui la précède.

Il y a aussi des autres mutations, par exemple; changer S en tS et mettre N, H ou T devant une voyelle. Ces "mutations" ne sont pas dans les catégories ci-dessus.

Les voyelles sont généralement comme au latin, mais elles ne sont pas claires quand elles ne sont pas sur la première syllabe. C'est sur la première syllabe que l'accent tombe dans la majorité des dialectes. Les diphthongues présentent des problèmes au début, mais elles se conforment à une formule.

11

Irish Mutation-Pronunciation Chart

b   + I,E = <u>b</u>eauty/<u>b</u>ien
bh + I,E = <u>v</u>iew/<u>v</u>iens
mb + I,E = <u>m</u>eow/<u>mi</u>eux

c   + I,E = <u>k</u>iosk/<u>q</u>uiet
ch + I,E = *NE/silent*
gc + I,E = *NE*

d   + I,E = <u>j</u>ob/a<u>dj</u>uger
dh + I,E = <u>y</u>ear/a<u>y</u>ant/*silent*
nd + I,E = o<u>ni</u>on/oi<u>gn</u>on

f   + I,E = <u>fj</u>ord/<u>f</u>ier
fh + I,E = <u>h</u>igh/<u>ha</u>-<u>ha</u>/*silent*
bhf + I,E = <u>v</u>iew/<u>v</u>iens

g   + I,E = *NE*
gh + I,E = <u>y</u>ear/a<u>y</u>ant/*silent*
ng + I,E = si<u>ng</u>/pi<u>ng</u>on

l   + I,E = <u>l</u>int/<u>l</u>e,<u>li</u>eu

m   + I,E = <u>m</u>eow/<u>mi</u>eux
mh + I,E = <u>v</u>iew/<u>v</u>iens

b   + A,O,U = <u>b</u>ox/<u>b</u>eau
bh + A,O,U = <u>v</u>at/<u>v</u>eau
mb + A,O,U = <u>m</u>ore/<u>m</u>on

c   + A,O,U = <u>c</u>all/<u>q</u>uant
ch + A,O,U = lo<u>ch</u>/lo<u>ch</u> *Écossais*
gc + A,O,U = <u>g</u>un/<u>g</u>omme

d   + A,O,U = <u>d</u>oor/<u>d</u>onc
dh + A,O,U = *NE/silent*
nd + A,O,U = <u>n</u>ot/<u>n</u>on

f   + A,O,U = <u>f</u>ire/<u>f</u>oux
fh + A,O,U = <u>h</u>ot/<u>ha</u>-<u>ha</u>/*silent*
bhf + A,O,U = <u>v</u>at/<u>v</u>eau

g   + A,O,U = <u>g</u>un/<u>g</u>omme
gh + A,O,U = *NE/silent*
ng + A,O,U = so<u>ng</u>/la<u>ng</u>ue

l   + A,O,U = <u>l</u>ake/<u>l</u>ong

m   + A,O,U = <u>m</u>ake/<u>m</u>ât
mh + A,O,U = <u>v</u>at,<u>w</u>ay/<u>v</u>eau,<u>ou</u>i

n	+ I,E = o<u>ni</u>on/oi<u>gn</u>on	
p	+ I,E = <u>pi</u>ano/<u>pi</u>astre	
ph	+ I,E = <u>fj</u>ord/<u>fi</u>er	
bp	+ I,E = <u>b</u>eauty/<u>bi</u>en	
r	+ I,E = <u>r</u>ear/<u>r</u>ire *(roulé)*	
s	+ I,E = <u>sh</u>ow/<u>ch</u>aud	
sh	+ I,E = *NE/H/silent*	
t	+ I,E = <u>ch</u>eek/<u>tch</u>èque	
th	+ I,E = *NE/H/silent*	
dt	+ I,E = <u>j</u>ob/a<u>dj</u>uger	

NE=no equivalent/pas d'équivalent

n	+ A,O,U = <u>n</u>ot/<u>n</u>on
p	+ A,O,U = <u>p</u>ot/<u>p</u>eau
ph	+ A,O,U = <u>f</u>ont/<u>f</u>aux
bp	+ A,O,U = <u>b</u>one/<u>b</u>as
r	+ A,O,U = <u>r</u>aw/<u>r</u>ond *(roulé)*
s	+ A,O,U = <u>s</u>ow/<u>s</u>on
sh	+ A,O,U = <u>h</u>ow/<u>ha</u>-<u>ha</u>/*silent*
t	+ A,O,U = <u>t</u>an/<u>t</u>aux
th	+ A,O,U = <u>h</u>ot/<u>ha</u>-<u>ha</u>/*silent*
dt	+ A,O,U = <u>d</u>oor/<u>d</u>onc

There are three types of consonant mutation:

1. **PALATALIZATION**=putting a narrow vowel I,E beside the consonant(s).
   or
   BROADENING=putting a broad vowel A,O,U beside the consonant(s).

2. **LENITION/ASPIRATION**=adding an H after it; i.e. changing D to DH.

3. **ECLIPSIS**=covering the consonant with another; i.e. changing D to an N sound. This is not shown by putting an N right beside the D as in Irish. For example; *nan doras* (of the doors) - some people will pronounce the *d* and some will change it to *n*. It is *na ndoras* in Irish.

Sometimes you will see a consonant or consonant cluster which has been dropped in speech.
It doesn't matter which side of the consonant the narrow or broad vowel touches; it affects the consonant or consonant cluster. If there are vowels on both sides of a consonant or consonant cluster, they both must be broad, or both be slender. For example, the *n* in *dùn* (a fort) is not the same as the *n* in *dùin* (of a fort), and notice that in the word *duine* (a person), it is a narrow vowel which comes after the *n*, since it is a narrow vowel which precedes it.

There are other mutations which happen, for example, S changing to t-S and a vowel having an N or H or T put in front of it. These "mutations" do not go under the above categories.

Vowels are vaguely like in Latin, but can become unclear if not on the first syllable. It is on the first syllable that the stress is put. Diphthongs present a problem at first, as they make quite different sounds, however even these follow a pattern.

B,D,G in the middle and at the end of words are voiceless and therefore sound like P,T,C respectively.

Il y a trois types de mutation consonantique:

1. **PALATISER**=mettre une voyelle frontale I,E à la consonne.

   ou

   DÉPALATISER=mettre une voyelle postérieure A,O,U à la consonne.

2. **LÉNIFIER**=mettre un H après; comme changer D en DH.

3. **ÉCLIPSER**=éclipser la consonne avec une autre; comme changer D en son N.

Ce n'est pas juste devant en touchant le D qu'on voit le N comme en irlandais. Par exemple; *nan doras* (des portes *[au génitif]*) - certains prononcent le *d* et les autres le changent en *n*. C'est *na ndoras* en irlandais.

On voit quelque fois une consonne ou un groupe de consonnes qui s'avale.

Peu importe quel côté la voyelle frontale ou la voyelle postérieure touche; elle affectue la consonne ou le groupe de consonnes. S'il y a des voyelles sur les deux côtés de la consonne ou du groupe de consonnes, il faut que les deux soient postérieures ou qu'elles soient frontales. Par exemple, le *n* en *dùn* (une fortresse *[au génitif]*) n'est pas le même *n* qu'en *dùin* (d'une fortresse). Voyez aussi que dans le mot *duine* (un homme), c'est une voyelle frontale qui suit le *n*, parce que c'est une voyelle frontale qui la précède.

Il y a aussi des autres mutations, par example; changer S en t-S ou mettre N, H ou T avant une voyelle. Ces "mutations" ne sont pas dans les catégories ci-dessus.

Les voyelles sont généralement comme en latin, mais elles ne sont pas toujours claires quand elles ne sont pas sur la première syllabe. C'est sur la première syllabe que l'accent tombe. Les diphthongues présentent des problèmes au début, mais elles se conforment à une formule.

B,D,G quand ils viennent au milieu des mots sont prononcés comme P,T,C respectivement.

Gaelic Mutation-Pronunciation Chart

b + I,E = <u>b</u>eauty/<u>bi</u>en
bh + I,E = <u>v</u>iew/<u>vi</u>ens
b can change to m / b peut se changer en m

c + I,E = <u>k</u>iosk/<u>qu</u>iet
ch + I,E = NE/silent
c can change to g / c peut se changer en g

d + I,E = <u>j</u>ob/ad<u>j</u>uger
dh + I,E = <u>y</u>ear/a<u>y</u>ant/silent
d can change to n / d peut se changer en n

f + I,E = <u>fj</u>ord/<u>fi</u>er
fh + I,E = <u>h</u>igh/<u>ha</u>-<u>ha</u>/silent
f can change to v / f peut se changer en v

g + I,E = NE
gh + I,E = <u>y</u>ear/a<u>y</u>ant/silent
g can change to ng / g peut se changer en ng

l + I,E = <u>l</u>int/<u>le</u>,<u>li</u>eu
m + I,E = <u>m</u>eow/<u>mi</u>eux
mh+ I,E = <u>v</u>iew/<u>vi</u>ens

b + A,O,U = <u>b</u>ox/<u>b</u>eau
bh + A,O,U = <u>v</u>at/<u>v</u>eau

c + A,O,U = <u>c</u>all/<u>qu</u>ant
ch + A,O,U = lo<u>ch</u>/lo<u>ch</u> Écossais

d + A,O,U = <u>d</u>oor/<u>d</u>onc
dh + A,O,U = NE/silent

f + A,O,U = <u>f</u>ire/<u>f</u>en
fh + A,O,U = <u>h</u>ot/<u>ha</u>-<u>ha</u>/silent

g + A,O,U = gun/gomme
gh + A,O,U = NE/silent

l + A,O,U = <u>l</u>ake/<u>l</u>ong
m + A,O,U = <u>m</u>ake/<u>m</u>ât
mh + A,O,U = <u>v</u>at/<u>v</u>eau

n	+ I,E = o<u>ni</u>on/oi<u>gn</u>on		*n*	+ A,O,U = <u>n</u>ot/<u>n</u>on	

p + I,E = <u>pi</u>ano/<u>pi</u>astre
ph + I,E = <u>fj</u>ord/<u>fi</u>er
p can change to b / p peut se changer en b

r + I,E = <u>r</u>ear/<u>ri</u>re *(roulé)*

s + I,E = <u>sh</u>ow/<u>ch</u>aud
sh + I,E = *NE/H/silent*

t + I,E = <u>ch</u>eek/<u>tch</u>èque
th + I,E = *NE/H/silent*
t can change to d / t peut se changer en d

NE=no equivalent/pas d'équivalent

p + A,O,U = <u>p</u>ot/<u>p</u>eau
ph + A,O,U = <u>f</u>ont/<u>f</u>aux

r + A,O,U = <u>r</u>aw/<u>r</u>ond *(roulé)*

s + A,O,U = <u>s</u>ow/<u>s</u>on
sh + A,O,U = <u>h</u>ow/<u>h</u>a-<u>h</u>a/*silent*

t + A,O,U = <u>t</u>an/<u>t</u>aux
th + A,O,U = <u>h</u>ot/<u>h</u>a-<u>h</u>a/*silent*

Pronouncing Welsh

Welsh is easy to read. Generally speaking, what you see is what you hear. Stress is put on the last syllable but one (the penultimate). Diphthongs in Welsh are easy. They are simply pronounced as the appear. TAIR (=three-feminine version), is pronounced TA-EER.

Le gallois est facile à lire. Généralement, vous entendez comme vous lisez. C'est sur la pénultième syllabe (l'avant-dernière) que l'accent tombe. Les diphthongues en gallois sont faciles. Elles se prononcent comme elles sont écrites. TAIR (=trois-au féminin), se prononce TA-IR.

The Alphabet L'Alphabet

	as in	*comme*
A	at	attend
B	boat	balle
C	cat	couple
CH	Scottish *loch*	*loch* en écossais
D	dog	doux
DD	the	*the* en anglais
E	end	les
F	of	veau
FF	off	fabrique
G	guest	gazoil
NG	sing	angle *(sans le g après)*
H	hat	ha-ha
I	feet	italien
J	job	adjuger
L	lake	lac
LL	*hissing sound*	*son siffler*
M	money	mousse
N	now	neuf
O	all	offre
P	piece	peau
PH	five	feu
R	*rolled,gutteral,etc*	*roulée,guttarale,etc*
RH	*no equivalent*	*pas d'équivalent*
S	sink	soie
SH	shirt	chien
T	tea	tache
TSH	chips	tchècque
TH	the	*the* en anglais
U	*1-deer*	1-dire
	2-like French U	2-U français
W	wet, food	oiseau,où
Y	1-year	1-yeux
	2-done	2-le

Vowels Voyelles

long/longues

gwl**a**d	country/pays
h**e**n	old/vieux
h**i**r	long/long
t**o**	roof/toit
s**w**	zoo/zoo
un	one/un
d**y**n	man/homme
m**ô**r	sea/mer
p**ê**l	ball/balle
t**â**n	fire/feu

short/courtes

m**a**m	mother/mère
p**e**ll	far/loin
inc	ink/encre
ll**o**n	happy/heureux
l**w**c	luck/chance
t**u**n	tin/boîte (alimentation)
c**y**n	before/avant
m**o**r	so,as/tellement,aussi … (que)
c**e**ll	cell/cellule
t**a**n	under,until/sous,jusqu'à

word/*mot*	**soft** *douce* his/*sa,* *son (à lui)*	**nasal** *nasale* my/ *ma, mon*	**aspirate** *aspirée* her/ *sa, son (à elle)*
P	B	MH	PH
pen	ei ben	fy mhen	ei phen
T	D	NH	TH
tad	ei dad	fy nhad	ei thad
C	G	NGH	CH
ci	ei gi	fy nghi	ei chi
B	F	M	
brawd	ei frawd	fy mrawd	- - -
D	DD	N	
drws	ei ddrws	fy nrws	- - -
G	- - - (silent)	NG	
gardd	ei ardd	fy ngardd	- - -
LL	L		
llyfr	ei lyfr	- - -	- - -
M	F		
mam	ei fam	- - -	- - -
RH	R		

Vowels (as well as consonants) can be long or short. Often if there are two consonants after it, the vowel will be short, and when there is one, the vowel will be long. Generally speaking, what you see is what you hear. Stress is put on the last syllable but one (the penultimate), and is very strong.

Les voyelles, aussi que les consonnes, peuvent être longues ou courtes. C'est souvent que la voyelle sera courte s'il y a deux consonnes après, et qu'elle sera longue s'il n'y a qu'une. Généralement, vous entendez comme vous lisez. C'est sur la pénultième syllabe (l'avant-dernière) que l'accent tombe, et l'accent est très fort.

The Alphabet L'Alphabet

	as in	*comme*
A	at	attend
B	boat	balle
C'H	house	ha-ha
CH	shirt	chien
D	dog	doux
E	end	les
F	five	feu
G	gun	gomme
H	silent	silent
I	feet	italien
J	Zha-Zha Gabor	juge
K	cat	couple
L	lake	lac
M	money	mousse
N	now	neuf
O	all	offre
P	piece	peau
R	*rolled, gutteral, etc*	*roulée, guttarale, etc*
S	sink	soie
T	tea	tache
U	*like in French*	tu
V	vine	vieux
W	wet, food	oiseau, où
Y	year	yeux
Z	zebra	zèbre

Breton Mutation Chart

word/*mot*	soft *douce* his/sa, son (à lui)	aspirate *aspirée* her/*sa,son* (à elle)	hard *dure* your/*votre*
P penn	B e benn	F he fenn	- - -
T tad	D e dad	Z he zad	- - -
K ki	G e gi	C'H he c'hi	- - -
B breur	V e vreur	- - -	P ho preur
D dor	Z e zor	- - -	T ho tor

G garzh	C'H e c'harzh	- - -	K ho karzh
M mamm	V e vamm	- - -	- - -
GW gwele	W e wele	- - -	KW ho kwele
GOU gouel	OU e ouel	- - -	KOU ho kouel

- - - = NO CHANGE/PAS DE CHANGEMENT

penn	= head/tête	garzh	= garden/jardin
tad	= father/père	mamm	= mother/mère
ki	= dog/chien	gwele	= bed/lit
breur	= brother/frère	gouel	= festival/fête
dor	= door/porte		

Lenition (Softening)
Lénition (Adoucissement)

B>V	Breizh	>da Vreizh	to Brittany/à Bretagne
D>Z	dorn	>e zorn	his hand/sa main (à lui)
G>C'H	glin	>e c'hlin	his knee/son genou (à lui)
Gw>W	gwele	>e wele	his bed/son lit (à lui)
Gou>Ou	gouelan	>e ouelan	his seagull/son goéland (à lui)
K>G	kador	>ar gador	the chair/la chaise
P>B	penn	>daou benn	two heads/deux têtes
T>D	tomm	>re domm	too hot/trop chaud(e)
M>V	moc'h	>e voc'h	his pigs/ses cochons (à lui)

Spirantisation (Aspirate)
Spirantisation (Aspirée)

K>C'H	ki	>ma c'hi	my dog/mon chien
P>F	penn	>he fenn	her head/sa tête (à elle)
T>Z	tad	>he zad	her father/son père (à elle)

Provection (Hardening)
Provection (Durcissement)

B>P	bro	>ho pro	your country, region/votre pays,région
D>T	dor	>ho tor	your door/votre porte
G>K	genoù	>ho kenoù	your mouth/votre bouche,votre gueule

Mixed
Mixte

B>V	bale	>o vale	walking around en train de se promener
M>V	mont	>o vont	going/en train d'aller
D>T	dont	>o tont	coming/en train de venir
G>C'H	gall	>ma c'hall X	if X can/si X peut
Gw>W	gwelet	>e welet	seeing him/le voir (masc.)
Gou>Ou	gouel	>da ouel X	to the festival of X/(aller) à la fête d'X

	as in	**comme**
A	at	attend
B	boat	balle
C'H	house	ha-ha
CH	shirt	chien
D	dog	doux
E	end	les
F	five	feu
G	gun	gomme
H	silent	silent
I	feet	italien
J	Zha-Zha Gabor	juge
K	cat	couple
L	lake	lac
M	money	mousse
N	now	neuf
O	all	offre
P	piece	peau
R	*rolled,gutteral,etc*	*roulée,guttarale,etc*
S	sink	soie
T	tea	tache
U	*like in French*	tu
V	vine	vieux
W	wet, food	oiseau,où
Y	year	yeux
Z	zebra	zèbre

greetings
cyfarchion
beannachtaí
beannachdan
gourc'hemennoù
saluer

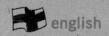 english	 welsh cymraeg gallois	 irish gaeilge irlandais
How are you?	Shwd dych chi?	Dé mar atá tú? / Cé mar atá tú? / Cén **ch**aoi bhfuil tú? / Conas atá tú? c>ch
I'm X.	X ydw i. *(Myfi X)*	Is mise X.
Who are you?	Pwy dych chi? / Pwy wyt ti?	Cé sibhse*? / Cé tusa? *plural only/pluriel seulement*
What is your <u>name</u>?	**B**eth yw dy <u>enw</u>? **B**eth yw eich <u>enw</u>? *= pa + peth*	Dé an **t-a**inm atá ort? Dé an **t-a**inm atá oraibh? a>t-a Cén **t-a**inm atá ort? Cén **t-a**inm atá oraibh? a>t-a Cad is <u>ainm</u> duit? Cad is <u>ainm</u> daoibh? *dé=goidé=cad é=cé*
What do you do for <u>a living</u>? **What is your <u>occupation</u>?**	Beth yw dy <u>**g**yrfa</u>/<u>**a**lwedigaeth</u>? g>_ Beth yw eich <u>gyrfa/ galwedigaeth</u>?	Goidé an **t-s**lí **bh**eatha atá agat? s>t-s, b>bh Goidé an **t-s**lí **bh**eatha atá agaibh*? s>t-s, b>bh *plural only/pluriel seulement*
I'm <u>a carpenter</u>.	<u>Saer</u>/<u>Saer coed</u> dwi.	<u>Saor</u> atá ionam/Is <u>saor</u> mé.

26

 gaelic **gàidhlig** gaélique	 breton **brezhoneg** breton	français
Dè mar a tha thu? Ciamar a tha thu? Cionnas a tha thu?	Mat an traoù ganeoc'h?	Ça va?
Is mise X.	X on.	Je m'appelle X.
Cò sibhse? / Cò thusa?	Piv oc'h? / Piv out?	Et vous? / Et toi?
Dè an **t-a**inm a tha ort? Dè an **t-a**inm a tha oirbh? a>**t-a**, _dè=gu dè=ciod e=cia_	Peseurt <u>anv</u> ac'h eus? Peseurt <u>anv</u> hoc'h eus?	Comment t'appelles-tu? Comment vous appelez-vous?
Dè an <u>cosnadh</u> a tha agad? Dè an <u>cosnadh</u> a tha agaibh?	Peseurt <u>micher</u> ac'h eus? Peseurt <u>micher</u> hoc'h eus?	Quel est ton <u>métier</u>? Quel est votre <u>métier</u>?
<u>Saor</u> a tha annam.	<u>Kalvez</u> on.	Je suis <u>menuisier/charpentier</u>.

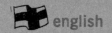 english	 welsh cymraeg gallois	irish gaeilge irlandais
<u>Where</u> are you <u>from</u>?	Un <u>o ble</u> dych chi? = <u>o + pa + ll</u>e	Carb as thú?
1. <u>Would you like</u> to …? *"you" singular/singulier*	1. <u>Wyt ti</u> eisiau …?	1. <u>Ar mh</u>aith leat …? m > mh
go for a walk go out to eat go window shopping	mynd am **d**ro mynd allan i **f**wyta mynd i **g**rwydro'r siopau t > d, b > f, c > g	dul amach ag siúl dul amach chun ithe dul amach ag siopadóireacht
2. (<u>Yes</u>,) with pleasure.	2. <u>Ydw</u>, â **ph**leser p > ph <u>Ydw</u>, ar **b**ob cyfrif p > b <u>Ydw</u>, yn llawen	2. <u>Ba mh</u>aith, cinnte. m > mh
2. <u>No</u>, thanks.	2. <u>Nac ydw</u>, diolch.	2. <u>Níor mh</u>aith, go raibh maith agat. m > mh; *níor=char*
It's <u>true</u>.	Mae'n <u>w</u>ir. g > _	Is <u>fíor</u> sin/Tá sin <u>fíor</u>.
That is <u>correct</u>.	Mae hynny yn **g**ywir. c > g	Is <u>ceart</u> sin/Tá sin <u>ceart</u>.
That is <u>incorrect</u>.	Mae hynny yn <u>anghywir</u>.	Is <u>mí-ch</u>eart sin Tá sin <u>mí-ch</u>eart. c > ch

28

 gaelic **gàidhlig** gaélique	breton **brezhoneg** breton	français
Cò as a tha sibh?	Eus pelec'h emaoc'h?	D'où est-ce que vous êtes?
1. Am bu toil leat …?	1. C'hoant ac'h eus da …?	1. Est-ce que tu voudrais…?
dol a-mach air sgrìob dol a-mach airson ithe dol a-mach do na bùthan	vont da vale vont da zebriñ vont da welout ar stalioù m>v, b>v, d>z>, gw>w	aller te promener aller manger aller faire du lèche-vitrine
2. Bu toil, cinnteach.	2. Ya, laouen.	2. (Oui,) avec plaisir.
2. Cha bu toil, tapadh leat.	2. Ne 'm eus ket, trugarez.	2. Non, merci.
Tha sin fìor.	Gwir eo.	C'est vrai.
Tha sin ceart.	Se zo reizh.	C'est correct ça.
Tha sin ceàrr.	N'eo ket reizh se.	C'est incorrect ça.

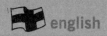 english	 welsh **cymraeg** gallois	irish **gaeilge** irlandais
O.K.	Iawn.	Ceart go leor.
That isn't <u>true</u>.	Dyw e **dd**im <u>yn **w**ir</u>. d>dd, g>_	Ní <u>**f**íor</u> sin Chan **fh**íor sin. f>fh
I hate <u>that</u>.	Mae'n **g**as gen i <u>hynny</u>. c>g; *gen i=gyda fi*	Is fuath liom <u>sin</u>.
Get out of here/Take off/ Go away!	Cer o 'ma/Dos o 'ma!	Gabh amach!
Thanks	Diolch	Go raibh maith agat/agaibh* *the plural is not used for the formal singular/on n'utilise pas le pluriel comme singulier polit*
Thank you very much	Diolch yn **f**awr iawn m>f	Go raibh míle maith agat/agaibh *agaibh=plural/pluriel*
You're welcome	Croeso/Iawn	Is é do **bh**eatha Is é bhur* **mb**eatha b>bh, b>mb *plural only/pluriel seulement*

30

 gaelic **gàidhlig** gaélique	 breton **brezhoneg** breton	français
Ceart gu leòr.	Mat eo.	**Correct.**
Cha eil sin <u>fìor</u>.	N'eo ket <u>gwir</u> se.	**Ce n'est pas <u>vrai</u> ça.**
Is fuath leam <u>sin</u> Is beag orm <u>sin</u> Is lugha orm <u>sin</u>.	Me am eus kaz ouzh <u>se</u>.	**Je hais <u>ça</u>.**
Gabh a-mach/A-mach leat/ Mach à seo/Thug do chasan leat	Kerzh/Kerzh kuit Kerzh da Bariz!	**Va-t-en!**
Tapadh leat/Tapadh leibh	Trugarez	**Merci**
Mòran taing	Trugarez **v**ras b>v	**Merci beaucoup**
Is e do **bh**eatha Is e bhur beatha b>bh	Netra/Mann bet	**De rien**

 english	 welsh cymraeg gallois	 irish gaeilge irlandais
Welcome to Brittany.	<u>Croeso</u> i **L**ydaw. **Ll**>**L**	<u>Fáilte</u> go dtí an **Bh**riotáin. **B**>**Bh**
Fair play <u>to him</u>.	Chwarae teg <u>iddo</u>.	Fair play <u>dhó</u>.
I like <u>that</u>.	Dwi'n licio <u>hynny</u>.	Is maith liom <u>sin</u>.
Stop/Stop that!	Paid!	Stop!
Hello.	Shw mae.	Dia dhuit.
Bye	Hwyl	Slán
Bye for now	Hwyl am y tro	Slán go fóill
Good night	Nos da	Oíche **mh**aith **m**>**mh**
See you <u>tomorrow</u>	Gwela i di <u>fory</u> Gwela i chi <u>fory</u>	Chífidh mé <u>amáireach</u> thú Chífidh mé <u>amáireach</u> sibh

 gaelic gàidhlig gaélique	breton brezhoneg breton	français
<u>Fàilte</u> don **Bh**reatainn **Bh**ig. B>Bh, B>Bh	<u>Degemer</u> mat e Breizh.	**<u>Bienvenue</u> en Bretagne.**
Math e fhèin!	*no equivalent/il n'y a pas d'équivalent*	*no equivalent/il n'y a pas d'équivalent*
Is toil leam <u>sin</u>.	<u>Se</u> a **b**lij din. p>b	**J'aime bien <u>ça</u>.**
Sguir!	Harz!	**Arrêt!**
Ciamar a tha sibh? Ciamar a tha thu?	Mat an traoù ganeoc'h?	**Bonjour.**
Tìridh an-dràsda	Kenavo	**Au revoir**
Tìridh an-dràsda	Ken ar **w**ech all g>_ Ken a vo gwelet	**À bientôt**
Oidhche **mh**ath m>mh	Noz **v**at m>v	**Bonne nuit**
Chì mi <u>a-màireach</u> thu Chì mi <u>a-màireach</u> sibh	Benn <u>warc'hoazh</u>	**À <u>demain</u>**

 english	 welsh cymraeg gallois	 irish gaeilge irlandais
Bye/Bye for now	Hwyl/Hwyl am y tro	Slán/Slán (leat/libh) Slán (agat/agaibh)
I'm sorry about that/Excuse me/ Pardon	Mae'n **dd**rwg gyda fi **d**>**dd**	Gabhaigí* mo leithscéal Gabh mo leithscéal *plural only/pluriel seulement*
You idiot!	Y twpsyn!	Amadáin!
You've got cheek! = *joue*	Mae gen ti wyneb! =*face/visage*	Nach ortsa atá an aghaidh! =*the face/le visage*

 gaelic **gàidhlig** gaélique	breton **brezhoneg** breton	français
Tìridh an-dràsda Beannachd (leat/leibh)	Kenavo/Ken ar wech all g>_	**Au revoir**
Gabhaibh mo lethsgeul Gabh mo lethsgeul	Eskuzit ac'hanon Eskuz ac'hanon	**Excusez-moi/Excuse-moi/Pardon**
Amadain!	Genaouek!	**Imbécile!**
Nach ann agad-sa a tha an aghaidh! *an agaidh=a'bhathais =the face/le visage*	Da **veg**! b>v *=your mouth/ta gueule*	**Ta gueule!** *= your mouth*

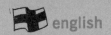 english	 welsh cymraeg gallois	 irish gaeilge irlandais
I'm sorry	Mae'n **dd**rwg gyda fi **d**>**dd**	Gabh mo leithscéal
I did it by mistake.	Camgymeriad gen i oedd hi.	Rinne mé de **dh**earmad é. **d**>**dh**
Pardon? Could you repeat that?	Mae'n **dd**rwg gyda fi. **W**newch chi ail**dd**weud hynny? **d**>**dd**, **G**>_, **d**>**dd**	Gabh mo leithscéal. Abair arís é más é do **th**oil é. **t**>**th**
I don't understand.	Dwi **dd**im yn deall. **d**>**dd**	Ní **th**uigim/Cha **dt**uigim. **t**>**th**, **t**>**dt**
I don't know.	Dwi **dd**im yn gwybod/**W**n i **dd**im/Sai'n gwybod. **d**>**dd**, **G**>_, **d**>**dd**	Níl a **fh**ios agam/Chan **fh**uil a **fh**ios agam. **f**>**fh**, **f**>**fh**, **f**>**fh**
<u>What</u> did you say?	<u>Beth</u> **dd**wedoch chi? **d**>**dd**	<u>Goidé</u> a dúirt sibh?
What did <u>you</u> say? *singulier familier*	Beth **dd**wedaist <u>ti</u>? **d**>**dd**	Goidé a dúirt <u>tú</u>? *dé=goidé=cad é*
What a <u>pity</u>/That's too bad!	Hen **d**ro/<u>Trueni</u> mawr! **t**>**d**	Nach mór an <u>trua</u>!

gaelic **gàidhlig** gaélique	breton **brezhoneg** breton	français
Gabh mo lethsgeul	Eskuzit ac'hanon	**Excusez-moi**
Cha robh mi a' ciallachadh a dhèanamh.	**D**re fazi am eus graet anezhañ. **T > D**	**Je ne l'ai pas fait exprès.**
Gabh mo lethsgeul. Abair a-rithist e mas e do **th**oil e. t>th	Eskuzit ac'hanon. Lavarit se un eil wech mar plij.	**Excusez-moi. Voulez-vous répéter?**
Chan eil mi a' tuigsinn.	Ne **g**omprenan ket. **k>g**	**Je n'ai pas bien compris.**
Chan eil **fh**ios agam. **f>fh**	N'ouzon ket/Ne ouian ket/Ne oaran ket.	**Je ne sais pas.**
<u>Dè</u> thuirt sibh?	<u>Petra</u> hoc'h eus lavaret?	<u>Qu'</u>avez-vous dit?
Dè thuirt <u>thu</u>? *dè=gu dè=ciod e*	Petra ac'h eus <u>lavaret</u>?	**Qu'as-<u>tu</u> dit?**
Nach mòr an <u>truaigh</u>!	Un **d**<u>ruez</u> eo! **t>d**	<u>**Dommage**</u>!

39

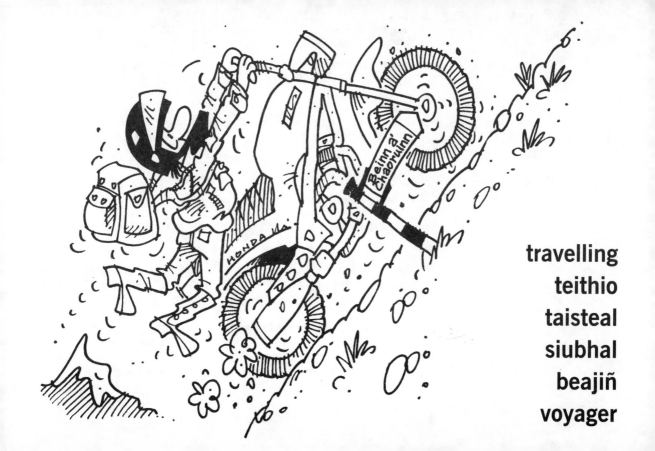

travelling
teithio
taisteal
siubhal
beajiñ
voyager

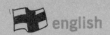 english	 welsh cymraeg gallois	irish gaeilge irlandais
We are looking for a <u>bed and breakfast</u> for tonight.	Dyn ni yn chwilio am <u>wely a brecwast</u> am y noson. g>_	Tá muid ag lorg <u>lóistín</u> le haghaidh na hoíche.
Let's stop driving for a while. I'm tired and <u>weak</u>.	Gwnawn ni stopio gyrru am ychydig. Dwi'n **f**linedig a <u>gwan</u>.	Stadaimid de **th**iomáint fad píosa. Tá mé tuirseach agus <u>fann</u>. t>th
It is not permitted <u>to camp</u> here.	Ni **ch**aniateir <u>gwersylla</u> yma. c>ch	Ní **ch**eadítear <u>campáil</u> anseo. c>ch
The <u>ship</u> sailed at night.	Hwyliodd y <u>llong</u> yn y nos.	**Sh**eol an <u>long</u> ar an oíche. S>Sh
Damn! I lost <u>five pounds</u> in this bloody gambling machine!	Damio! Dwi wedi colli <u>pum punt</u> yn y blydi peiriant gamblo 'ma.	Diabhail! Tá <u>cúig **ph**unt</u> caillte san inneal **ch**luiche seo agam! p>ph, c>ch

<u>Did he go</u> to London last night with John?
   yes
   no
	<u>A aeth e</u> i **L**undain neithiwr gyda Siôn? Ll>L
	   do
	   naddo (na)
		<u>An **nd**eachaigh sé</u> go Londain aréir le Seán? d>nd
		   chuaigh
		   ní **dh**eachaigh
		   d>dh

 gaelic gàidhlig gaélique	 breton brezhoneg breton	français
Tha sinn a' lorg <u>leabaidh is breacaist</u> airson na h-oidhche.	Ni zo o klask <u>lojeiz</u> evit an nozvez/Ni zo o klask <u>bod ha boued</u> evit an nozvez.	**Nous cherchons une <u>chambre d'hôte</u> pour ce soir.**
Stadamaid a **dh**raibheadh airson greiseig. Tha mi sgìth agus <u>fann</u>. **d>dh**	Deomp d'ober un ehan e pad ur pennadig. Skuizh ha <u>gwann</u> on.	**Arrêtons quelques minutes. Je suis <u>fatigué(e)</u>.**
Chan eil cead <u>campadh</u> an seo.	Difennet eo <u>kampiñ</u> amañ.	**<u>Le camping</u> n'est pas permis ici.**
Sheol an <u>long</u> feadh na h-oidhche. **S>Sh**	Treuzet he deus ar <u>**v**atimant</u> e pad an noz. **b>v**	**Le <u>bâteau</u> a traversé pendant la nuit.**
A **Dh**iabhail! Tha <u>còig puinnd</u> caillte agam san inneal **ch**luiche seo! **D>Dh, c>ch**	Kaoc'h/Gast! Kollet am eus <u>pemp lur saoz</u> er **c'h**ozh mekanik-c'hoari-mañ! **k>c'h**	**Merde! J'ai perdu <u>cinq livres</u> dans cette putain de machine à sous à la con!**
<u>An deach e</u> gu Lunnain an-raoir còmhla ri Seonaidh? chaidh cha deach *an deach=an deachaidh*	<u>Aet oa</u> dec'h d'an noz da Londrez gant Yann? ya ne oa ket	**<u>Est-ce qu'il est allé</u> à Londres hier soir avec Jean?** **oui** **non**

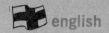 english	 welsh cymraeg gallois	irish gaeilge irlandais
We will be meeting them <u>on Wednesday</u>.	Byddwn ni yn cwrdd â nhw **dd**ydd Mercher. d>dd	Beidh muid ag cruinniú <u>Dé Céadaoin</u> leo.
Will the boat be leaving <u>at ten</u>?	(Ai) am **dd**eg y bydd y cwch yn gadael? d>dd	(An) <u>ar a deich</u> a bheas an bád ag fágáil?
yes	ie	is ea
no	nage	ní h-ea (chan ea)
Your <u>passport</u> please.	Eich <u>pasport</u> os gwelwch yn **dd**a. d>dd	Do **ph**as más é do **th**oil é. p>ph, t>th
What is your <u>surname</u>?	**B**eth yw eich <u>cyfenw</u>? = *pa + peth*	Goidé an <u>sloinne</u> atá ort*? *=*singular only/singulier seulement*
What is your <u>address</u>?	**B**eth yw eich <u>cyfeiriad</u>? = *pa + peth*	Goidé an <u>seoladh</u> atá agat*? *=*singular only/singulier seulement*
<u>What</u> do you do?	**B**eth yw eich gwaith? = *pa + peth*	<u>Goidé</u> an obair atá agat? *goidé an=cén*

gaelic gàidhlig gaélique	breton brezhoneg breton	français
Bidh sinn a' coinneachadh <u>Diciadain</u> riutha.	En em **g**avout raimp ganto (benn) <u>dimerc'her</u>. **k>g**	**Nous les rencontrerons <u>mercredi</u>.**
<u>(An ann) aig a deich</u> a bhios an aiseag a' fàgail? is ann chan ann	<u>Da **z**ek eur</u> e vo ar **v**atimant o **v**ont? **d>z, m>v** ya n'eo ket	**Est-ce que c'est <u>à dix heures</u> que le bâteau partira?** oui non
Ur <u>cead dol thairis</u> mas e'r toil e.	Ho <u>tremen-hent</u> mar plij.	**Votre <u>passeport</u> s'il vous plaît.**
Dè an <u>sloinneadh</u> a tha oirbh*? *ort=singular/singulier	Peseurt <u>anv familh</u> hoc'h eus?	**Quel est votre <u>nom de famille</u>?**
Dè an <u>seòladh</u> a tha agaibh? agad=singular/singulier	Peseurt <u>chomlec'h</u> hoc'h eus?	**Quelle est votre <u>adresse</u> (s'il vous plaît)?**
<u>Dè</u>'n obair a tha agaibh?	<u>Peseurt</u> labour hoc'h eus?	**<u>Quel</u> est votre travail?**

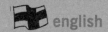 english	 welsh cymraeg gallois	 irish gaeilge irlandais
I am <u>a doctor</u> / a teacher / *a businessman* / a student.	<u>Meddyg</u> / athro / *dyn busnes* / myfyriwr **ydw i**.	<u>Dochtúir</u> / múinteoir / *fear gnó* / mac léinn **atá ionam**.
What is the purpose of your <u>visit</u>?	**B**eth yw bwriad y <u>d</u>aith yma? = *pa + peth*, **t>d**	Goidé atá d'intinn agat* ar an <u>turas</u> seo? *singular only/ singulier seulement*
vacation business smuggling cocaine	gwyliau busnes smyglo cocên	laethanta saoire <u>gnó</u> smugláil cóicéin
Do you intend to stay more <u>than three months</u>? maybe	Ydi hi'n **f**wriad gyda chi i aros yn hirach <u>na tri mis</u>? **b>f** efallai	An bhfuil súil agat le fanacht níos faide <u>ná trí **mh**í</u>? **m>mh** b'**fh**éidir **f>fh**
<u>How much</u> money have you got? *"you" plural/"vous" pluriel*	**F**aint o arian sy gyda chi? **M>F** *(=pa + maint)*	<u>Cé **mh**éad</u> airgid atá agaibh? **m>mh**
Two thousand <u>five hundred</u> dollars. $2,500	Dwy **f**il <u>pum can</u> doler. **m>f** $2,500 *can=cant*	Dhá **mh**íle <u>cúig **ch**éad</u> dollar. **m>mh, c>ch** $2,500

46

gaelic gàidhlig gaélique	breton brezhoneg breton	français
is e <u>dotair</u> / tidsear / *fear gnothaich* / oileanach **a tha annam**.	<u>Mezeg</u> / kelenner / *den aferioù* / studier **on**.	Je suis <u>docteur</u> / professeur / *homme d'affaires* / étudiant.
Dè tha an inntinn agaibh air an <u>turas</u> seo?	Petra eo mennad ar <u>v</u>eaj-mañ ganeoc'h? **b>v**	Quel est le bout de votre <u>visite</u>?
làithean saora <u>gnothach</u> cùl-mhùtaireachd coicèin	vakañsoù <u>aferioù</u> floderezh kokaen	vacances <u>affaires</u> passer du cocaïne en contrebande
A' bheil sibh am beachd fuireach nas **fh**aide <u>na trì mìosan</u>? dh' **fh**aodadh **f>fh**	Ar mennad zo deoc'h da chom hiroc'h <u>eget tri mizvezh</u>? marteze	Est-ce que vous comptez rester plus <u>de trois mois</u>? peut-être
<u>Cia **mh**eud</u> airgid a tha agaibh? **m>mh**	<u>Pegement</u> arc'hant zo ganeoc'h?	<u>Combien</u> d'argent avez-vous apporté?
Dà **mh**ìle <u>còig ceud</u> dolair. **m>mh** $2,500	Daou **v**il <u>pem kant</u> dollar. **m>v** $2.500	Deux mille <u>cinq cents</u> dollars. $2.500

47

in the car
yn y car
sa charr
sa chàr
er c'harr
en voiture

 english	 welsh cymraeg gallois	irish gaeilge irlandais
<u>Which</u> is the way to X Town?	<u>Beth</u> yw'r ffordd i **D**re X? = *pa* + *peth*, **T** > **D**	<u>Goidé</u> an **t-s**lí go Baile X/<u>Cad é</u> an taobh go Baile X? **s** > **t-s**
<u>There</u>'s the tourist information centre.	<u>Dyna</u>'r **g**anolfan **w**ybodaeth i ymwelwyr. **c** > **g**, **g** > _	<u>Sin</u> oifig an Bhoird Fháilte.

Would you like to rent/hire <u>a</u> car?
    yes
    no
	Wyt ti am hurio <u>car</u>?
	
	    ydw
	    nac ydw (na)
		Ar **mh**aith leat <u>carr</u> a **th**ógáil ar cíos?
		    ba **mh**aith
		    níor **mh**aith (char **mh**aith)
		    m > **mh**, **t** > **th**

Drive carefully	Gyrrwch yn **o**falus. **g** > _	Aire ar an **bh**óthar. **b** > **bh**

<u>Welcome</u> to England.
    England ENG
	<u>Croeso</u> i **G**ymru.
	    Cymru **CYM**
		<u>Fáilte</u> go h-Éirinn.
		    Éire **IRL**

Damn! We missed the exit for the M4!	Damio! Dyn ni wedi colli'r allanfa i'r M4!	Diabhail! Tá muid i **nd**iaidh an **t-s**lí amach don M4 a **ch**ailliúnt! **d** > **nd**, **s** > **t-s**, **c** > **ch**
James! <u>Where</u> is the map?	Iago! **B**le mae'r map? *pa* + *lle*	A **Sh**éamais! <u>Cáit</u> a bhfuil an mapa? **S** > **Sh**, *cáit=cá*

50

 gaelic **gàidhlig** gaélique	breton **brezhoneg** breton	français
Dè an rathad gu Baile X? Dè an taobh gu Baile X?	Da beseurt tu emañ Kêr X? p>b	**Quelle** est la route de la Ville X?
Sin an oifis don luchd-turais.	Setu burev an douristed. t>d	**Voilà** le syndicat d'initiative.
Am bu toil leat càr a ghabhail air mhàl? bu toil cha bu toil g>gh, m>mh	C'hoant ac'h eus da feurmiñ ur c'harr? ya ne m'eus ket k>c'h	**Est-ce que** tu veux louer une voiture? oui non
Thoiribh an aire air an rathad.	Diwallit war an hent.	**Conduisez** prudemment.
Fàilte gu h-Albainn. Alba **SC**	Degemer mat e Breizh. Breizh **BZH**	**Bienvenue** en France. France **F**
A Dhiabhail! Leig sinn seachad an dol-a-mach don M4! D>Dh	Kaoc'h! Manket hon eus ar sorti d'an M4!	**Bordel de merde!** Nous avons manqué la sortie pour le M4!
A Sheumais! Càit a bheil am mapa? S>Sh, *càit=cà*	Jakez! Pelec'h emañ ar gartenn? k>g	**Jacques!** Où est la carte?

51

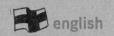 english	welsh cymraeg gallois	irish gaeilge irlandais
James will not be buying petrol tomorrow.	Fydd Iago ddim yn prynu petrol yfory. **B>F, d>dd**	Ní bheidh Séamas ag ceannacht peitreal amáireach. **b>bh,** *Ní=Cha*
Where is the <u>nearest</u> petrol station?	Ble mae'r orsaf betrol <u>agosaf</u>? **g>_, p>b**	Cáit a bhfuil an garáiste <u>is giorra</u> orainn?
NO PARKING	DIM PARCIO	TÁ COSC AR **PH**ÁIRCEÁIL **P>PH**
X will be <u>going</u> by car.	Yn y car y bydd X <u>yn mynd</u>.	(Is) sa **ch**arr a bheas X <u>ag dul</u>. **c>ch**
Remember to drive <u>on the left/ on the right</u>.	Cofiwch yrru <u>ar y chwith/ar y **dd**e</u>. **g>_, d>dd**	Cuimhnígí tiomáint <u>ar an taobh **ch**lí/ar an taobh deis</u>. **c>ch**
<u>Why</u> is the blue Honda doing 60 km in the inside lane?	<u>Pam</u> y mae'r Honda glas yn gwneud 60 km yn y lôn **f**ewnol? **m>f**	<u>Cén fáth</u> atá an Honda gorm ag déanamh 60 km sa lána laistigh?
<u>A mile</u> is 1.609 kilometres.	1.609 cilometr yw <u>milltir</u>.	Is 1.609 ciliméadar é <u>míle</u> 1.609 ciliméadar atá i <u>míle</u> Is é 1.609 ciliméadar <u>míle</u>.

gaelic gàidhlig gaélique	breton brezhoneg breton	français
Cha **bh**i Seumas a' ceannachd peatroil a-màireach. **b>bh**	Ne **b**reno ket Jakez eoul-maen warc'hoazh. **p>b**	**Jacques n'achetera pas d'essence demain.**
Càit a bheil an garaids <u>as **fh**aisg</u> oirnn?	Pelec'h emañ ar **c'h**arrdi <u>tostañ</u>? **k>c'h**	**Où est la station-service <u>la plus proche</u>?**
NA PÀRCAIBH	ARABAT GARIÑ	**STATIONNEMENT INTERDIT**
(Is e/Is ann) sa **ch**àr a bhios X <u>a' dol</u>. **c>ch**	Er **c'h**arr e vo X <u>o **v**ont</u>. **k>c'h, m>v**	**X <u>ira</u> en voiture.**
Cuimhnichibh draibheadh <u>air an taobh **ch**lì/air an taobh **dh**eas</u>. **c>ch, d>dh**	Dalc'hit soñj bleniañ <u>war an tu kleiz/war an tu dehou</u>.	**Gardez votre <u>gauche/droite</u>.**
<u>Carson</u> a tha an Honda gorm a' deanamh 60km san lòn luath?	<u>Perak</u> e ra an Honda glas 60 km er gwenodenn **v**uan? **b>v**	**<u>Pourquoi</u> la Honda bleue ne fait que du 60 km sur la voie rapide?**
Is e 1,609 cilemeatair a tha ann am mìle.	<u>Ur miltir</u> zo 1,609 kilometr/<u>Ur mil saoz</u> zo 1,609 kilometr.	**<u>Un mile</u> vaut 1,609 kilomètres.**

53

 english	 welsh cymraeg gallois	 irish gaeilge irlandais
20 litres of <u>unleaded</u> please.	20 litr o'r <u>di-**b**lwm</u> os gwelwch yn **dd**a. p>b, d>dd	20 lítear den <u>an-luaidh</u> más é do **th**oil é. t>th
We should check the <u>oil</u>.	Dylen ni edrych ar yr <u>olew</u>.	Ba **ch**óir dhúinn súil a **th**abhairt ar an <u>ola</u>. c>ch, t>th
No smoking	Dim smygu	Cosc ar **th**obac Cosc ar **ch**aitheamh t>th, c>ch

 gaelic **gàidhlig** gaélique	breton **brezhoneg** breton	français
20 litear den <u>an-luaidhe</u> mas e do* **th**oil/bhur toil e. **t**>**th,** *do=singular/singulier*	20 litrad <u>di-**b**lom</u> mar plij. **p**>**b**	**20 litres de <u>(super) sans plomb</u> s'il vous plaît.**
Bu **ch**òir dhuinn sùil a **th**oirt air an <u>ola</u>. **c**>**ch**, **t**>**th**	Gwelloc'h e vefe gwiriañ an <u>eoul.</u>	**C'est la peine de vérifier l'<u>huile</u>.**
Na smocaibh	Arabat butuniñ	**Défense de fumer**

bus and train
bws a trên
bus agus traen
bus agus trèan
karr boutin ha treñ
bus et train

 english	 welsh cymraeg gallois	irish gaeilge irlandais
What time does it arrive?	Faint o'r gloch mae'n cyrraedd? M>F (=pa + maint), c>g	Goidé an uair atá sé ag teacht?
ARRIVALS DEPARTURES	CYRRAEDD YMADAEL	TEACHTAÍ IMEACHTAÍ
Did you go to the duty-free shop? yes no	Est ti i'r siop ddi-doll? do naddo (na) d>dd, t>d	An ndeachaigh tú go dtí an siopa saor ó dhleacht? chuaigh ní dheachaigh d>nd, d>dh
I want a ticket to Shanghai, please.	Tocyn i Shanghai os gwelwch yn dda. d>dd	Ticéad go Shanghai más é do thoil é. t>th
a single ticket/a one way ticket a return ticket	tocyn unffordd tocyn dwyffordd	ticéad singil ticéad fillte
We are waiting in a train station.	Dyn ni'n aros mewn gorsaf drenau. t>d	Tá muid ag feitheamh i stáisiún traenach. in=before a vowel/ avant la voyelle
Where is the hotel?	Ble mae'r gwesty?	Cáit a bhfuil an óstlann?

 gaelic **gàidhlig** gaélique	breton **brezhoneg** breton	français
<u>Dè an uair</u> a tha e a' tighinn? *tighinn = teachd*	<u>Da **b**et eur</u> e teuio? p > **b**	<u>À quelle heure</u> arrive-t-il?
A' RUIGHEACHD A' FALBH	DONEDIGEZHIOÙ KIMIADOÙ	**ARRIVÉES** **DÉPARTS**
An deach thu don **bh**ùth <u>sh</u>aor o <u>ch</u>ìsean cusbainn? chaidh cha deach b > **bh**, s > **sh**, c > **ch**	Aet out d'ar boutik <u>kuit-a-gargoù</u>? ya n'on ket k > **g**	**Est-ce que tu est allé(e) au magasin <u>hors-taxes</u>?** oui non
<u>Ticeid</u> gu Shanghai mas e bhur toil e.	<u>Ur bilhed</u> evit Shanghai mar plij.	<u>Un billet</u> **pour Shanghai s'il vous plaît.**
ticeid <u>singilte</u> ticeid <u>tillidh</u>	bilhed <u>mont hepken</u> bilhed <u>mont-dont</u>	**un billet <u>aller simple</u>** **un billet <u>aller-retour</u>**
Tha sinn a' feitheamh <u>ann an</u> stèisean trèanaichean.	Ni zo o **c'h**ortoz <u>en un</u> ti-gar. g > **c'h**	**Nous attendons <u>dans une</u> gare.**
Càit a bheil an <u>taigh-òsda</u>? *taigh = tigh*	Pelec'h mañ an <u>osteleri</u>?	**Où est l'<u>hôtel</u>?**

 english	 welsh cymraeg gallois	 irish gaeilge irlandais
Let's put up <u>the tent</u>.	Gwnawn ni **o**sod y **b**abell. g>_, p>b	Cuirimis suas <u>an puball</u>.
The people next door are making <u>a lot</u> of noise.	Mae'r **b**obl drws nesa yn gwneud <u>llawer</u> o sŵn. **p>b**	Tá na daoine sa **ch**éad seomra eile ag déanamh <u>go leor</u> fuaime. **c>ch**
X will be going <u>by plane</u>.	<u>Yn yr awyren</u> y bydd X yn mynd.	<u>(Is e) san eitleán</u> a bheas X ag dul.
When is the bus <u>coming</u>?	Pryd mae'r bws <u>yn dod</u>?	Cathain atá an bus <u>ag teacht</u>?

 gaelic **gàidhlig** gaélique	breton **brezhoneg** breton	français
Cuireamaid suas <u>an teanta</u>. *an teanta=am puball*	Deomp da sevel <u>an **d**eltenn</u> t>d	**Montons <u>la tente</u>.**
Tha na daoine san ath-**sh**eòmar a' dèanamh <u>gu leòr</u> a dh'**fh**uaim. s>sh, f>fh	An **d**ud e-kichen zo oc'h ober <u>kalz</u> a **d**rouz. t>d, t>d	**Les gens à côté font <u>beaucoup de bruit</u>.**
<u>(Is ann) sa **ph**lèan</u> a bhios X a' dol. p>ph	<u>En ur **c'h**arr-nij</u> e yelo X. k>c'h	**<u>C'est en avion</u> que X voyagera.**
Cuin a tha am bus <u>a' tighinn</u>?	Pegoulz e vo ar bus <u>o **t**ont</u>? d>t	**Quand est-ce que le bus <u>arrive</u>?**

sports
chwaraeon
cluichí
cluichean
sportoù
sport

 english	 welsh cymraeg gallois	 irish gaeilge irlandais
swimming	nofio	snámh
Playing football/soccer.	Chwarae pêl-droed. t>d	Ag imirt sacair.
rugby	rygbi	rugbaí
wrestling	reslo/codymo	coraíocht
The hotel has a tennis court.	Mae cwrt tenis yn y gwesty.	Tá faiche leadóige san óstlann.
climbing	dringo	an dreapadóireacht
hiking	cerdded	siúl
boots	sgidiau/bwtsias	bróga
rope	rhaff	rópa
mountain	mynydd	sliabh
moor	rhos	móinteach/sliabh
promontory	pentir/penrhyn/trwyn	ceann tíre/rinn/ros
view	golygfa	radharc/adharc
We are looking for a map of public footpaths.	Dyn ni'n chwilio am fap o'r llwybrau cyhoeddus. m>f	Tá muid ag lorg mapa de na cosáin phoiblí. p>ph

gaelic gàidhlig gaélique	breton brezhoneg breton	français
snàmh	neuial	nager
A' cluich ball-coise.	O c'hoari mell-**d**road. t>d	Jouer au foot.
rugbaidh	rugbi	rugby
carachd	gouren	lutte
Tha <u>cùirt leadaige</u> san taigh-òsda.	<u>Un **d**achenn **d**ennis</u> a zo gant an ostaleri. t>d, t>d	Il y a <u>un terrain de tennis</u> à l'hôtel.
an streapadh	pignad	escalade
coiseachd	tro-**v**ale b>v	randonnée
brògan/bòtannan	boutoù	bottes
ròpa	kordenn	corde
beinn	menez	montagne
monadh/mòinteach	lanneg	lande
ceann tìre/rinn/ros/sròn	beg-douar	promontoire
sealladh/radharc/fradharc	gwel	vue
<u>Tha sinn a' lorg</u> mapa de na cas-**sh**lighean poblach. s>sh	<u>Klask a reomp</u> ur **g**artenn eus ar gwenodennoù boutin. k>g	<u>Nous cherchons</u> une carte des sentiers publics.

65

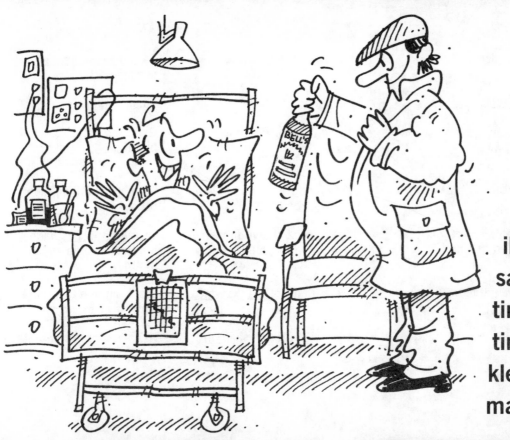

illness
salwch
tinneas
tinneas
kleñved
maladie

 english	welsh cymraeg gallois	irish gaeilge irlandais
She is <u>sea-sick</u>.	Mae <u>salwch môr</u> arni hi.	Tá <u>tinneas na mara/tinneas na farraige</u> uirthí.
He has <u>a cold</u>.	Mae <u>annwyd</u> arno fe.	Tá <u>slaghdán</u> air.
Where is <u>the chemist</u>, please? *chemist=pharmacy*	Esgusodwch fi. Ble mae<u>'r fferyllfa</u>?	Gabh mo leithscéal. Cáit a bhfuil <u>an cógaslann</u>? *cógaslann=siopa poitigéara*
<u>I think</u> my toe is broken.	<u>Dwi'n meddwl</u> fy mod i wedi torri bys troed.	<u>Sílim</u> go bhfuil an méar coise briste orm.
<u>I hope</u> we don't get food poisoning in this hole.	<u>Gobeithio</u> na <u>ch</u>awn ni <u>w</u>enwyn bwyd yn y twll yma. c>ch, g>_	<u>Tá mé i nd</u>óchas nach nimheofar muid san áit seo. d>nd
Bring some vitamin C <u>in the suitcase</u>.	Dere â fitamin C <u>yn y siwtces</u>.	Bíodh vitimín C <u>sa mh</u>ála taistil agat. m>mh
<u>They are</u> in the waiting room.	Yn y stafell aros <u>y maen nhw</u>.	(Is) san fheithealann <u>atá siad</u>.

 gaelic **gàidhlig** gaélique	breton **brezhoneg** breton	français
Tha <u>tinneas na mara/tinneas na fairge</u> oirre.	<u>Droug-mor</u> zo warni.	**Elle a <u>le mal de mer</u>.**
Tha <u>fuachd</u> air.	<u>Ur sifern</u> zo gantañ.	**Il a <u>un rhume</u>.**
Gabhaibh mo lethsgeul. Càit a bheil <u>bùth a' phoitigeir</u>?	Eskuzit ac'hanon. Pelec'h emañ an <u>apotiker</u>?	**Excusez-moi. Où est <u>la pharmacie</u>?**
<u>Saoilidh mi</u> gun do **bh**ris mi mo ladhar. **b**>**bh**	<u>Me gav din</u> em eus torret ma biz-troad.	**<u>Je pense</u> que je me suis cassé l'orteil.**
<u>Tha mi an dòchas</u> nach bi sinn air ar puinnseanachadh san àite seo.	<u>Esperout ran</u> ne vimp ket ampoezoned en toull-mañ.	**<u>J'espère</u> qu'on ne se fera pas empoisonner dans ce trou.**
Biodh bhiotamain C <u>sa **mh**à</u>ileid agad. **m**>**mh**	Digas vitamin C ganit <u>er **v**alizenn</u>. **m**>**v**	**Apporte de la vitamine C <u>dans la valise</u>.**
(Is ann) san **t-s**eòmar feithimh <u>a</u> tha iad. **s**>**t-s**	Er sal **c'h**ortoz <u>emaint</u>. **g**>**c'h**	**<u>Ils sont</u> dans la salle d'attente.**

69

emergencies
argyfwng
cruachás
cruaidh-chàs
enkadennoù
urgences

english	welsh cymraeg gallois	irish gaeilge irlandais
Where is <u>the hospital</u>?	Ble mae<u>'r ysbyty</u>?	Cá bhfuil <u>an **t-o**spidéal</u>? **o>t-o**, *cá=cáit*
You will need <u>stitches</u>.	Mae angen cael <u>pwythau</u> arnoch chi.	Caithfidh tú <u>greamanna</u> a **fh**áil. **f>fh**
We had an <u>accident</u> **with the car.**	Dyn ni wedi cael <u>damwain</u> gyda'r car.	Bhain <u>timpiste</u> dhúinn leis an **ch**arr. **c>ch**
We have a flat tyre. *tyre=tire*	Dyn ni wedi cael twll yn y teiar.	Tháinig poll ar an **bh**onn. **b>bh**
Where is the <u>tavern</u>?	Ble mae'r <u>tafarn</u>?	Cáit a bhfuil an <u>teach tábhairne</u>?

72

 gaelic gàidhlig gaélique	breton brezhoneg breton	français
Cà bheil <u>an **t-o**spadal</u>? **o>t-o**, *cà=càit*	Pelec'h emañ <u>an ospital</u>?	**Où est <u>l'hôpital</u>?**
Tha ort <u>grèimeannan</u> a **fh**aighinn. **f>fh**	Ezhomm po <u>gwrioù</u>.	**Il vous faut des <u>sutures</u>.**
Bha <u>tubaist</u> againn leis a' **ch**àr. **c>ch**	<u>Un darvoud</u> hon eus bet gant ar **c'h**arr. **k>c'h**	**On a eu <u>un accident</u> avec la voiture.**
Thàinig toll air a' **bh**onn. **b>bh**	Un dic'hwez hon eus bet.	**On a crevé.**
Càit a bheil <u>an taigh-òsda</u>?	Pelec'h emañ an **d**avarn? **t>d**	**Où est le <u>bar</u>?**

73

shopping
siopa
sa mhargadh
sa mhargadh
er marc'had
les courses

 english	 welsh cymraeg gallois	irish gaeilge irlandais
Saturday is <u>market-day</u> in this town.	Dydd Sadwrn yw <u>diwrnod y farchnad</u> yn y **d**re yma. m>f, t>d	Is é An Satharn <u>lá an **mh**argaidh</u> sa **bh**aile seo. m>mh, b>bh
Look! Leather <u>shoes</u> for three hundred francs.	Drycha! <u>Sgidiau</u> lledr am **d**ri **ch**an ffranc. t>d, c>ch	Féach! <u>Bróga</u> leathair ar **th**rí **ch**éad franc. t>th, c>ch
<u>Maybe</u> there is a good clothes shop nearby.	<u>Efallai</u> bod siop **dd**illad **dd**a yn agos. d>dd, d>dd	B'**fh**éidir go bhfuil siopa éadaigh maith in aice linn. f>fh
<u>Look</u>! There is a sale over here.	<u>Drycha</u>! Mae sêl yma.	<u>Féach</u>! Tá saor-reic anseo.
X and Y <u>credit cards</u> are accepted here.	Derbynnir <u>cardiau credyd</u> X ac Y yma.	Glactar le <u>cairteanna creidmheasa</u> X agus Y anseo.
Let the <u>buyer</u> beware.	Gocheled y <u>prynwr</u>.	Rabhadh don **ch**eannaitheoir. c>ch

 gaelic **gàidhlig** gaélique	breton **brezhoneg** breton	🍷 français
Is e Disathairne <u>là a' **mh**argaidh</u> sa **bh**aile seo. m>mh, b>bh	Ar Sadorn eo <u>deiz ar marc'had</u> er **g**êr-mañ. k>g	**C'est le samedi <u>le jour du marché</u> dans cette ville.**
Seall! <u>Brògan</u> leathair air tri ceud franc. *seall=feuch*	Sell! <u>Botoù</u> laer evit tri **c'h**ant lur. k>c'h	**Regarde! <u>Chaussures</u> en cuir pour trois cent francs.**
<u>Dh'**fh**aodadh</u> gu bheil bùth aodaich **mh**ath faisg oirnn. f>fh, m>mh	<u>Marteze</u> ez eus ur boutik dilhad mat e-kichen.	**<u>Peut être</u> qu'il y a un magasin de vêtements non loin.**
<u>Seall</u>! Tha saor-reic an seo. *seall=feuch*	<u>Sell</u>! Ur **w**erzh zo amañ. g>_	**<u>Regarde</u>! Il y a des soldes.**
Gabhar ri <u>cairtean creideis</u> X agus Y an seo.	Degemeret vez <u>kartennoù kredit</u> X hag Y amañ.	**Nous acceptons <u>les cartes de crédit</u> X et Y ici.**
Rabhadh don **ch**eannaichear. c>ch	Diwall d'ar <u>prenour</u>.	**Caveat <u>emptor</u>. (Avertissement à l'<u>acheteur</u>)**

the weather
y tywydd
an aimsir
an aimsir
an amzer
le temps

 english	welsh cymraeg gallois	irish gaeilge irlandais
It is <u>sunny</u> in the south.	Mae'n <u>heulog</u> yn y de.	Tá <u>grian ann</u> sa deisceart.
There was <u>a storm</u> last night.	Roedd <u>storm</u> neithiwr.	Bhí <u>doineann</u> ann aréir.
We will need good weather tomorrow.	Bydd angen tywydd braf arnon ni yfory.	Beidh soineann ag teastáil uainn amáireach.

 gaelic **gàidhlig** gaélique	breton **brezhoneg** breton	🍷 français
Tha <u>grian ann</u> mu **dh**eas. d>dh	Emañ <u>oc'h ober heol</u> er **c'h**reisteiz. k>c'h	**Il y a <u>du soleil</u> au sud.**
Bha <u>doineann</u> ann a-raoir.	<u>Un arnev</u> a oa dec'h d'an noz.	**Il y avait <u>un orage</u> hier soir.**
Bidh sìde **mh**ath a **dh**ìth oirnn a-màireach. m>mh, d>dh	Ezhomm amzer brav vo warc'hoazh.	**Il nous faudra du beau temps demain.**

signs
arwyddion
fógraí
sanasan
arouezioù
la signalisation

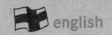 english	 welsh cymraeg gallois	irish gaeilge irlandais
one-way street	stryd unffordd	sráid aontreo
way in/entrance	i mewn/ffordd i mewn/mynedfa	isteach/slí isteach
exit/way out	allan/ffordd allan	amach/slí amach
emergency exit	allanfa frys/allanfa argyfwng b>f	bealach éalaithe
no smoking	dim smygu	cosc ar thobac/cosc ar chaitheamh t>th, c>ch
fire escape/fire exit	allanfa dân t>d	éalú teine
no parking	dim parcio	cosc ar pháirceáil p>ph
TELEPHONE	TELEFFÔN	TEILEAFÓN
Bed and Breakfast	Gwely a Brecwast/Llety	Lóistín
CAMPING	GWERSYLLA	CAMPÁIL

 gaelic **gàidhlig** gaélique	 breton **brezhoneg** breton	français
<u>sràid</u> aon rathad	<u>straed</u> un-tu	<u>rue</u> à sens unique
dol-a-steach/a-steach	e-barzh/mont-e-barzh/hent da **v**ont-tre m>v	entrée
dol-a-mach/a-mach	maez/mont-er-maez	sortie
doras-èiginn	toull-diankiñ	sortie de secours
na smocaibh	arabat butuniñ	défense de fumer
<u>teàrnadair</u>-o-**th**eine t>th	<u>toull</u> diankiñ	<u>sortie</u> de secours
na pàrcaibh	arabat gariñ	défense de stationner
TELEFÒN	PELLGOMZ	TÉLÉPHONE
Leabaidh is Breacaist	Boued ha Bod/Leti	Chambre d'hôte/Gîte
CAMPACHADH	KAMPIÑ	CAMPING

 english	 welsh cymraeg gallois	 irish gaeilge irlandais
north	gogledd	tuaisceart
south	de	deisceart,deis
east	gorllewin	iarthar
west	dwyrain	oirthear
town <u>centre</u>	<u>canol</u> y **d**ref t>d	an <u>lár</u>/lár an **bh**aile b>bh
city centre	canol y **dd**inas d>dd	lár na cathrach
customs	y **d**oll t>d	custam
bridge <u>closed</u>	pont <u>ar gau</u>	droichead <u>dúnta</u>
<u>open</u> between 8am and 10pm	<u>ar agor</u> rhwng 8 y bore a 10 yr hwyr **c**>**g**	<u>ar oscailt</u> idir a 8 sa **mh**aidin agus a 10 san oíche m>mh
toilets	toiledau	leithris
men/women	dynion/merched	fir/mná
Airport	Maes awyr	Aerphort
warning – wild boars – stop	rhybudd – moch gwyllt – stop	rabhadh – toirc allta – stad/stop

 gaelic **gàidhlig** gaélique	breton **brezhoneg** breton	français
tuath	an hanternoz/nórz	nord
deas	ar **c'h**reisteiz/su k>c'h	sud
iar/siar	reter/ar sav-heol	est
ear/sear	kornog/ar **c'h**uzh-heol k>c'h	ouest
<u>meadhan</u> a' **bh**aile b>bh	<u>kreiz</u>-kêr	<u>centre</u> ville
meadhan a' **bh**aile b>bh	kreiz-kêr	centre ville
cusbainn	maltouterezh	la douane
drochaid <u>dùinte</u>	pont <u>serret</u>	pont <u>fermé</u>
<u>fosgailte</u> eadar a 8 sa **mh**adainn	<u>digoret</u> etre 8 eur diouzh ar	<u>ouvert</u> entre 8 heures du matin
agus a 10 san oidhche m>mh	mintin ha 10 eur da'n noz	et 10 heures du soir
goireasan	privezioù	toilettes
fir/mnathan	gwazed/merc'hed	hommes/femmes
Port-Adhair	Aerborzh	Aéroport
rabhadh – tuirc alluidh – stad	diwall – moc'h gouez – arsavit	attention – sangliers – arrêt/stop

 english	welsh cymraeg gallois	irish gaeilge irlandais
Gaelic spoken here.	Siaredir Gaeleg yma.	Tá Gaeilge na h-Alban againn anseo. A>h-A
Irish language and welcome.	Gwyddeleg a chroeso. c>ch	GAEILGE AGUS FÁILTE.
I speak Breton.	Dwi'n siarad Llydaweg.	Tá an Bhriotáinis agam. B>Bh
do not enter pedestrian zone	peidiwch â mynd i mewn parth cerddwyr	ná téigh isteach/ná gabh isteach bealach coise
shopping centre	canolfan siopa	ionad siopadóireachta/ceantar siopaí
supermarket	archfarchnad	ollmhargadh
construction ahead	gwaith adeiladu o'ch blaen = *in front of you/devant vous*	obair thógála romhaibh t>th =*in front of you/devant vous*
polluted water do not swim	dŵr wedi'i lygru ll>l ni chaniateir nofio c>ch	uisce truaillte ní cheadaítear snámh c>ch
slippery surface falling rocks	ffordd lithrig l>ll cerrig yn syrthio	bóthar sleamhain carraigeacha ag titim

 gaelic gàidhlig gaélique	breton brezhoneg breton	français
THA GÀIDHLIG AIR A BRUIDHINN AN SEO.	Gouezeleg komzet amañ.	**On parle gaélique ici.**
Gàidhlig-Èirinn agus fàilte.	Iwerzhoneg ha degemer mat.	**Langue irlandaise et la bienvenue.**
Tha a' Bhreatannais agam. B>Bh	KOMZ A RAN BREZHONEG.	**Je parle breton.**
na teirig isteach/na gabh isteach rathad coise	arabat mont e-barzh parzh tud-war-droad t>d	**défense d'entrer zone pédestre**
ionad bhùthan b>bh	kreizenn-genwerzh k>g	**centre commercial**
mòr-bhùth b>bh	gourvarc'had	**hypermarché/supermarché**
obair thogail romhaibh t>th =*in front of you* / *devant vous*	labour hent en ho raok =*in front of you* / *devant vous*	**travaux en avant**
uisge truaillte na snàmh an seo	dour saotraet arabat neuial	**eau polluée défense de se baigner**
rathad sleamhainn creagan a' tuiteam	hent risklus karregoù o kouezhañ	**surface glissante chute de pierres**

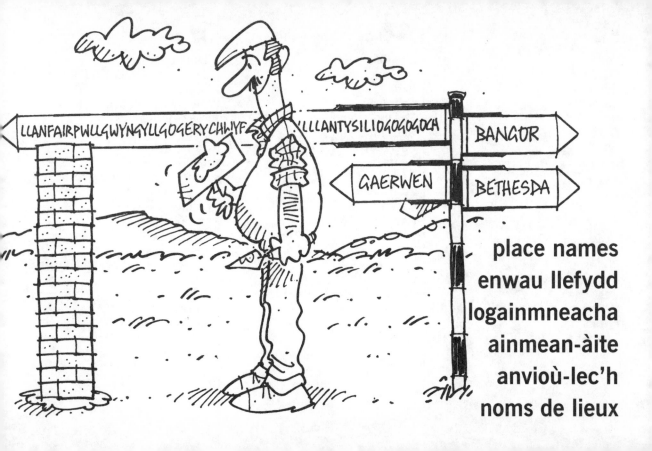

place names
enwau llefydd
logainmneacha
ainmean-àite
anvioù-lec'h
noms de lieux

 english	 welsh cymraeg gallois	 irish gaeilge irlandais
London	Llundain	Londain
Dublin	Dulyn	Baile Átha Cliath *(Duibhlinn)*
Paris	Paris	Páras
Cardiff	Caerdydd	Caerdydd/Cardiff
Rennes	Roazhon/Rennes	Roazhon/Rennes
Glasgow	Glaschu	Glaschú
Edinburgh	Caeredin	Dún Éideann
Belfast	Belffast	Béal Feirste/Béal Feirsde
Derry	Derry	Doire (**Ch**olm Cille) C>Ch
Cork	Corc	Corcaigh
Galway	Galway	Gaillimh
Rome	Rhufain	an Róimh
England	Lloegr	Sasana/Sasainn
Wales	Cymru	An **Bh**reatain **Bh**eag B>Bh, B>Bh
Ireland	Iwerddon	Éire
Scotland	Yr Alban	Albain
Brittany	Llydaw	An **Bh**riotáin B>Bh
France	Ffrainc	An **Fh**rainc F>Fh

 gaelic gàidhlig gaélique	 breton brezhoneg breton	français
Lunnainn	Londrez	**Londres**
Baile Àtha Cliath	Dulenn	**Dublin**
Paris	Pariz	**Paris**
Caerdydd/Cardiff	Kerdiz	**Cardiff**
Roazhon/Rennes	Roazhon	**Rennes**
Glaschu	Glaschu/Glasgw	**Glasgow**
Dùn Èideann	Din-Edin/Edimbourg	**Edimbourg**
Beul Feirsde	Béal Feirste/Belfast	**Belfast**
Doire **Ch**aluim **Ch**ille C>Ch	Doire/Derry	**Derry**
Corcaigh	Korkig/Cork	**Cork**
Gaillimh	Gaillimh/Galway	**Galway**
an Ròimh	Roma	**Rome**
Sasainn	Bro-Saoz	**Angleterre**
A' **Ch**uimrigh C>Ch	Kembre/Bro-**G**embre K>G	**Pays de Galles**
Èirinn	(Bro-) Iwerzhon	**Irlande**
Alba	(Bro-) Skos	**Écosse**
A' **Bh**reatainn **Bh**eag B>Bh	Breizh	**Bretagne**
An **Fh**raing F>Fh	Bro-**C'h**all G>C'h	**France**

food
bwyd
bia
biadh
boued
alimentation

 english	 welsh cymraeg gallois	 irish gaeilge irlandais
I'm hungry.	Mae <u>eisiau bwyd</u> arna i. *there is <u>the need of food</u> on me / il y a du <u>besoin de nourriture</u> sur moi*	Tá <u>an t-o</u>cras orm/Tá <u>ocras</u> orm. **o>t-o** *<u>the hunger</u> is on me, there is <u>hunger</u> on me / <u>la faim</u> est sur moi, il y a <u>de la faim</u> sur moi*
I'm thirsty.	Mae <u>syched</u> arna i. *there is <u>thirst</u> on me / il y a <u>de la soif</u> sur moi*	Tá <u>tart</u> orm. *there is <u>thirst</u> on me / il y a <u>de la soif</u> sur moi*
What do you want to <u>eat</u>? *"you" singular familiar/singulier familier*	**B**eth wyt ti eisiau ei **f**wyta? *= pa + peth,* **b>f**	Céard a ba **mh**aith leat <u>ithe</u>? **m>mh**
<u>Mary</u>! Where are the crisps and the coke?	<u>Mair</u>! Ble mae'r creision a'r coke?	A **Mh**áire! Cáit a bhfuil na brioscáin agus an coke? **M>Mh**
A loaf and four croissants <u>please</u>.	Torth a **ph**edwar croissant <u>os gwelwch yn **dd**a</u>. **p>ph, d>dd**	Builín agus ceithre croissant <u>más é do **th**oil é</u>. **t>th**
In the Lake View Hotel <u>restaurant</u>.	Ym **m**wyty Gwesty Golygfa'r Môr. *bwyty=tŷ bwyta* **b>m**	I **mb**ialann Óstán Radharc na Mara. **b>mb**

 gaelic **gàidhlig** gaélique	 breton **brezhoneg** breton	français
Tha an **t-a**cras orm/Tha <u>acras</u> orm. a>t-a *<u>the hunger</u> is on me,there is <u>hunger</u> on me / <u>la faim</u> est sur moi,il y a <u>de la faim</u> sur moi*	<u>Naon</u> am eus. *I have <u>hunger</u>*	**J'ai <u>faim</u>.** *I have <u>hunger</u>*
Tha <u>am pathadh</u> orm. *<u>the thirst</u> is on me / <u>la soif</u> est sur moi*	<u>Sec'hed</u> am eus. *I have thirst / J'ai soif*	**J'ai <u>soif</u>.**
Dè bu toil leat r'a <u>ithe</u>?	Petra ac'h eus c'hoant da **z**ebriñ? d>z	**Qu'est-ce que tu veux <u>manger</u>?**
A **Mh**àiri! Càit a bheil na briosgaidean agus an coke? M>Mh	**V**ari! Pelec'h mañ ar chips hag ar **c'h**oka? M>V, k>c'h	**<u>Marie</u>! Où sont les chips et le coca?**
Lòf agus ceithir croissants <u>mas e'r toil e</u>.	Un **d**orzh ha pevar kroasañ <u>mar plij</u>. t>d	**Un pain et quatre croissants <u>s'il vous plaît</u>.**
Ann an <u>taigh-bidhe</u> **Th**igh Òsda **Sh**ealladh na Mara. T>Th, S>Sh	E <u>ti-debri</u> Ostaleri Gwel ar Mor.	**Au <u>restaurant</u> de l'Hôtel Vue de la Mer.**

english	welsh cymraeg gallois	irish gaeilge irlandais
Have you reserved a <u>table</u>/Do you have a reservation?	Oes <u>bwrdd</u> ar gadw gyda chi?	Ar **ch**uir tú <u>bord</u> in áirithe? c>**ch**

Is this table <u>free</u>?
   yes
   no
	Ydi'r bwrdd yma <u>yn rhydd</u>?
	   ydi
	   nac ydi/nac yw
		An bhfuil an bord seo <u>saor</u>?
		   tá
		   níl/chan fhuil

Could you pass the <u>salt</u>/sugar/ketchup?
   yes
   no
	Wnewch chi **b**asio'r <u>halen</u>/siwgr/saws coch?
	   gwnaf
	   na **w**naf **G**>_, **p**>**b**, **g**>_
		An sínfidh tú chugam an <u>salann</u>/siúcra/citseap?
		   sínfidh
		   ní **sh**ínfidh/cha **sh**ínfidh **s**>**sh**

<u>A table</u> for two.	<u>Bwrdd</u> i **dd**au. **d**>**dd**	<u>Bord</u> do **bh**eirt/<u>Bord</u> do **dh**íst. **b**>**bh**, **d**>**dh**

<u>Some tea</u>?
   Yes
   No
	<u>Te</u>?
	   Oes
	   Nac oes (na)
		Ar **mb**eidh <u>tae</u> agat?
		   Beidh
		   Ní **bh**eidh (Cha **bh**eidh)
		   b>**mb**, **b**>**bh**

I like it <u>strong</u>/weak.	Dwi'n ei licio fe'<u>n g</u>ryf/**w**an. **c**>**g**, **g**>_	Is maith liom <u>láidir</u>/lag é.

A bheil <u>bòrd</u> glèidhte agaibh?	C'hwi hoc'h eus miret un <u>d</u>aol? t>d	**Avez-vous réservé une <u>table</u>/ Avez-vous une réservation?**

A bheil am bòrd seo <u>saor</u>?
  tha
  chan eil
	An **d**aol-mañ zo <u>dieub</u>?
	  ya
	  n'eo ket t>d
		**Cette table est-elle <u>libre</u>?
		  oui
		  non**

An sìn thu an <u>salann</u>/siùcar/
ceitseap?
  sìnidh
  cha **sh**ìn s>sh
	Deuit din gant an <u>holen</u>/sunkr/
	ketchup mar plij.
		**Passez le <u>sel</u>/sucre/ketchup s'il
		vous plaît.**

<u>Bòrd</u> do **dh**ithist. d>dh	<u>Un d</u>aol evit daou. t>d	**<u>Une table</u> pour deux.**

An gabh thu <u>tì</u>?
  Gabhaidh
  Cha **gh**abh g>gh
	<u>Te</u> az po?
	  Ya
	  N' am bo ket
		**<u>Du thé</u>?
		  Oui
		  Non**

Is toil leam <u>làidir</u>/lag e.	Te <u>kreñv</u>/gwan a **b**lij diñ. p>b	**Je l'aime <u>fort</u>/léger.**

99

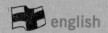 english	welsh cymraeg gallois	irish gaeilge irlandais
Herring and potatoes is <u>a speciality</u> in the Western Isles.	<u>Pryd arbennig</u> yw sgadan a tatws yn Ynysoedd y Gorllewin.	<u>Béile ar leith</u> atá i scadán is prátaí in Inse **Gh**all. **G>Gh**
X will be with us at the restaurant <u>tonight</u>.	Bydd X yn y tŷ bwyta gyda ni <u>heno</u>. *tŷ bwyta=bwyty*	Beidh X sa **bh**ialann in éineacht linn <u>anocht</u>. **b>bh**
<u>This</u> is broken. *neuter/neutre*	Mae <u>hon</u> wedi torri. *hon=feminine/féminin*	Tá <u>seo</u> briste. *seo=neuter/neutre*

Do you have <u>another chair</u>?
    yes
    no
	Oes <u>cadair arall</u> gyda chi?
	    oes
	    nac oes (na)
		An bhfuil <u>cathaoir eile</u> agaibh?
		    tá
		    níl (chan fhuil)

Ask the waiter for <u>the menu</u>.	Gofyn i'r gweinydd am y **f**wydlen. **b>f**	Iarr ar an **fh**reastalaí chun <u>an biachlár</u> a **fh**áil. **f>fh**
<u>What</u> are *you* eating?	<u>Beth</u> wyt *ti*'n ei **f**wyta? **b>f**	<u>Goidé</u> atá *tusa* ag ithe?
The place is closed <u>on Sundays</u>.	Bydd y lle ar **g**au <u>ar y Sul</u>. **c>g**	Bíonn an áit dúnta <u>ar an Domhnach</u>.
The food is <u>very good</u>.	Mae'r bwyd yn **dd**a iawn. **d>dd**	Tá an bia <u>an-**mh**aith</u>. **m>mh**

gaelic
gàidhlig gaélique

breton
brezhoneg breton

français

gàidhlig	brezhoneg	français

Lòn sònraichte a tha ann an sgadan is buntàta anns na **h-E**ileanan Siar. **E>h-E**

Ur pred ispisial eo harenk gant avaloù-douar en Enezioù ar **c'h**uzh 'heol. **k>c'h**

L'hareng avec les pommes de terre est <u>une spécialité</u> aux Western Isles.

Bidh X san taigh-bidhe còmhla ruinn <u>a-nochd</u>.

X vo en ti-debriñ ganeomp <u>fenoz</u>.

X sera avec nous au restaurant <u>ce soir</u>.

Tha <u>seo</u> briste.
seo=neuter/neutre

<u>Honnez</u> zo torret.
feminine/féminin

<u>Celle-là</u> est cassée.
feminine/féminin

A bheil <u>cathair eile</u> agaibh?
   tha
   chan eil

Ur **g**ador all hoc'h eus?
   ya
   ne m' eus ket **k>g**

Avez-vous <u>une autre chaise</u>?
   oui
   non

Iarr air an **fh**rithealaiche <u>an clàr bidhe</u> a **th**oirt dhuit. **f>fh, t>th**

Goulenn <u>ar **g**artenn</u>. **k>g**

Demande <u>le menu/la carte</u>.

<u>Dè</u> tha *thusa* ag ithe?

Petra a **z**ebrez-*te*? **d>z**

<u>Qu'est-ce</u> que tu manges *toi*?

Bidh an **t-à**ite dùinte <u>Didòmhnaich</u>. **à>t-à**

Serret **v**ez al lec'h <u>d'ar Sul</u>. **b>v**

L'endroit est fermé <u>le dimanche</u>.

Tha am biadh glè **mh**ath.
m>mh

Ar boued zo <u>mat-tre</u>.

La bouffe est <u>très bonne</u>.

101

 english	welsh cymraeg gallois	irish gaeilge irlandais
I like <u>ice cream</u>.	Dwi'n licio <u>hufen iâ</u>.	Is maith liom <u>uachtar reoite</u>.
Meals served <u>all day</u>.	Prydau o **f**wyd ar **g**ael **d**rwy'r <u>dydd</u>. b>f, c>g, t>d	Bia ar fáil <u>fad an lae</u>.
I am <u>a vegetarian</u>.	<u>Llysieuwr</u> ydw i.	<u>Feoilséantóir</u> atá ionam Is <u>feoilséantóir</u> mé.

 gaelic **gàidhlig** gaélique	breton **brezhoneg** breton	🍷 français
Is toil leam <u>uachdar reoite</u>.	<u>Dienn-skorn</u> a **b**lij diñ. p>b	J'aime <u>la glace</u>.
Biadh ri **fh**aighinn <u>fad an là</u>. f>fh	Boued servijet <u>an devezh pad</u>.	Mets servis <u>toute la journée</u>.
<u>Glasraichear/lusanach</u> a tha annam.	<u>Vejetarian</u> on/<u>Debrer-glasrez</u> on.	Je suis <u>végétarien</u>.

103

drink
diod
deoch
deoch
evaj
boissons

 english	welsh **cymraeg** gallois	irish **gaeilge** irlandais
We would like to see <u>the wine list</u>.	Hoffem ni **w**eld y rhestr <u>**w**inoedd</u>. g>_ , g>_	Ba **mh**aith linn <u>clár an **fh**íona</u> a **fh**eicsint. m>mh, f>fh, f>fh
A pint of <u>cider</u> please.	Peint o <u>seidr</u> os gwelwch yn **dd**a. d>dd	Pionta <u>ceirtlise</u> más é do **th**oil é. t>th
I'll have <u>a whisky</u> please.	<u>Chwisgi</u> os gwelwch yn **dd**a. d>dd	<u>Uisce beatha</u> más é do **th**oil. t>th
We sell <u>wine</u> and beer.	Gwerthir <u>gwin</u> a **ch**wrw yma. c>ch	Tá <u>fíon</u> agus leann ar díol anseo.
Do you have <u>red wine</u>? yes no	Oes <u>gwin coch</u> gyda chi? oes nac oes (na)	An bhfuil <u>fíon dearg</u> agaibh? tá níl (chan fhuil)

Welsh speakers! "Gwin coch" sounds like "shit wine" in Breton!

Aux galloisants! "Gwin coch" en gallois a le même son que "du vin merdique" en breton!

Bu toil leinn <u>clàr an **fh**ìona</u> a **fh**aicinn. f>fh, f>fh	Plijout a rafe deomp gwelout <u>listenn ar gwinioù</u>.	**Nous voudrions voir <u>la liste des vins</u>.**
Pinnt <u>leann-ubhail</u> mas e do **th**oil e. t>th	Ur (chopinad) <u>chistr</u> mar plij. **pint mesurement (=0.57 litre) not used on continent*	**Un <u>cidre</u> s'il vous plaît.** ****on n'utilise pas la pinte (=0,57 litre) au continent***
<u>Uisge beatha</u> mas e do **th**oil e. t>th	<u>Ur c'hwiski</u> mar plij.	**Un <u>whisky</u> s'il vous plaît.**
Tha <u>fìon</u> agus leann 'gan reic an seo.	<u>Gwin</u> ha bier e gwerzh amañ.	**<u>Vin</u> et bière en vente ici.**

A' bheil <u>fìon dearg</u> agaibh?
  tha
  chan eil
	<u>Gwin ruz</u> hoc'h eus?
	  ya
	  ne m' eus ket
		Avez-vous <u>du vin rouge</u>?
		  oui
		  non

 english	 welsh cymraeg gallois	irish gaeilge irlandais
We will be blind drunk <u>tonight</u>.	Byddwn ni yn meddwi'n **d**wll <u>heno</u>. **t>d**	Beidh muid dallta leis an ól <u>anocht</u>.
I have a <u>hangover</u>.	Mae gennyf fi **b**enmaenmawr. **p>b**	Tá <u>an fuíoll galair</u> orm.
Cheers!	Iechyd da!	Sláinte/Sláinte **mh**aith! **m>mh**

gaelic	breton	français
Bidh sinn air ar dalladh leis an deoch <u>a-nochd</u>.	Mezv dall e vimp <u>fenoz</u>.	**On va se bourrer la gueule <u>ce soir</u>.**
Tha <u>ceann-daoraich</u> orm.	<u>Poan v</u>lev am eus. **b>v**	**J'ai une <u>gueule de bois</u>.**
Slàinte/Slàinte **mh**òr/Slàinte **mh**ath! **m>mh**	Yec'hed mat!	**Santé!**

in the hotel
yn y gwesty
san óstán
san taigh-òsda
en ostaleri
à l'hôtel

 english	 welsh cymraeg gallois	irish gaeilge irlandais
At the reception desk	Wrth y **dd**esg **g**roesawu d>dd, c>g	San **fh**áiltiú f>fh
Do you have any rooms <u>available</u>?	Oes stafell <u>ar **g**ael</u> gyda chi? c>g	An bhfuil seomra <u>ar fáil</u> agaibh?
<u>**What kind**</u> of room do you want? *"you" plural/"vouz" pluriel*	<u>Pa **f**ath</u> o stafell dych chi am ei **g**ael? m>f, c>g	<u>Cén sórt</u> seomra a ba mhaith libh?
A double <u>room</u>.	<u>Stafell</u> **dd**wbl. d>dd	<u>Seomra</u> dúbailte.
<u>**Here**</u> is the conference room.	<u>Dyma</u>'r stafell **g**ynadleddau. c>g	<u>Seo</u> an seomra comhdhála.
I'll see you in the <u>dining room</u>.	Gwela i di yn y <u>stafell **f**wyta</u>. b>f	Feicfidh mé sa <u>seomra bia</u> thú. *feicfidh=chí=tchífidh*
<u>**The lift**</u> is broken. We will have to take the stairs. *lift=elevator*	Mae<u>'r lifft</u> wedi torri i lawr. Bydd yn rhaid i ni **f**ynd i fyny'r grisiau. m>f	Tá <u>an t-a</u>rdaitheoir briste. Caithfidh muid dul suas an staighre. a>t-a
Where is the <u>hotel</u>?	Ble mae'r <u>gwesty</u>?	Cáit a bhfuil an **t-ó**stán? ó>t-ó

112

 gaelic **gàidhlig** gaélique	 breton **brezhoneg** breton	français
San ionad-fàilte	Ouzh an degemer	**À la réception/À l'accueil**
A bheil seòmar <u>ri **fh**aighinn</u> agaibh? f>fh	Ur **g**ambr zo <u>dieub</u> ganeoc'h? k>g	**Avez-vous des chambres <u>disponibles</u>?**
<u>Dè seòrsa</u> seòmar a bu toil leibh?	<u>Peseurt</u> kambr a **b**lijfe deoc'h? p>b	**<u>Quel type</u> de chambre désirez-vous?**
<u>Seòmar</u> dùbailte.	<u>Ur **g**ambr</u> evit daou. k>g	**<u>Une chambre</u> pour deux.**
<u>Seo</u> an seòmar co-labhairt.	<u>Setu</u> sal an emguzuliañ.	**<u>Voilà</u> la salle des conférences.**
Chì mi san **t-s**eòmar-bidhe thu. s>t-s	En em **w**elout a rin ganez er <u>sal-debriñ</u>. gw>w	**Je te reverrai à la <u>salle à manger</u>.**
Tha <u>an **t-à**rdaichear</u> briste. Feumaidh sinn dol suas an staidhre. à>t-à	<u>Ar pignerez</u> zo torret. Ret vo deomp kemer an diri.	**<u>L'ascenseur</u> est en panne. Il nous faudra prendre l'escalier.**
Càit a bheil an <u>taigh-òsda</u>?	Pelec'h emañ an <u>ostaleri</u>?	**Où est l'<u>hôtel</u>?**

 english	 welsh cymraeg gallois	 irish gaeilge irlandais
The toilets are at the end of the corridor.	Ym mhen y coridor y mae'r toiledau. p>mh	(Is) i gceann an bhealaigh atá na leithris. c>gc, b>bh
Ladies Gents	Merched Dynion	Mná Fir
toilets	toiledau y tŷ bach=*the small house/la petite maison* y lle chwech=*the "six" place/l'endroit "six"*	leithris an teach beag=*the small house/la petite maison* teach an asail=*the donkey's house/la maison de l'âne*
There is no hot water!	Does dim dŵr poeth!	Níl uisce te ann!
What time is breakfast?	Am faint o'r gloch y mae'r brecwast? M>F *(=pa + maint)*, c>g	Cén uair atá an bricfeasta?
The people next door are making a lot of noise.	Mae'r bobl drws nesa yn gwneud llawer o sŵn. p>b	Tá na daoine sa chéad seomra eile ag déanamh go leor fuaime. c>ch
I have to go to the toilet.	Rhaid i fi fynd i'r tŷ bach. m>f	Caithfidh mé dul go dtí an teach beag.

114

 gaelic gàidhlig gaélique	 breton brezhoneg breton	français
(Is ann) aig ceann an trannsa a tha na goireasan.	E penn an trepas emañ ar privezioù.	**Les toilettes** sont au bout du couloir.
Mnathan/Boireannaich Fir	Merc'hed Gwazed	**Femmes** **Hommes**
goireasan an taigh beag=*the small house/ la petite maison*	privezioù	**toilettes**
Chan eil uisge teth ann!	N'eus ket dour tomm!	Il n'y a pas d'eau chaude!
Dè'n uair a tha am breacaist?	Da bed eur emañ al lein? p>b	C'est à quelle heure le petit déjeuner?
Tha na daoine san ath-sheòmar a' dèanamh gu leòr a dh'fhuaim. s>sh, f>fh	An dud e-kichen zo oc'h ober kalz a drouz. t>d, t>d	Les gens d'à côté font beaucoup de bruit.
Tha agam ri dhol don taigh bheag/Feumaidh mi dol don taigh bheag. d>dh, b>bh	Ret eo din mont d'ar privezioù.	J'ai besoin d'aller aux toilettes.

 english	welsh **cymraeg** gallois	irish **gaeilge** irlandais
We want to make <u>a long distance call</u>.	Dyn ni am **w**neud <u>galwad **b**ell</u>. g>_, p>b	Ba **mh**aith linn <u>glaoch aistear fada</u> a **ch**ur. m>mh, c>ch
We are <u>now</u> in the Irish-speaking area.	Yn y **f**ro **W**yddeleg dyn ni <u>nawr</u>. b>f, G>_	(Is) sa **Gh**aeltacht atá muid <u>anois</u>. G>Gh
<u>The people of the area</u> are friendly.	Mae <u>pobl yr ardal</u> yn **g**yfeillgar. c>g	Tá <u>muintir na **h-á**ite</u> cairdiúil Is cairdiúil <u>muintir na **h-á**ite</u>. á>h-á

Bu toil leinn <u>glaodh astar fada</u> a **ch**ur. **c>ch**	C'hoant hon eus d'ober <u>un taol pellgomz a-**b**ell</u>. **p>b**	Nous voulons (on veut) faire <u>un appel longue distance</u>.
(Is ann) sa **Gh**àidhealtachd a tha sinn <u>a-nis</u>. **G>Gh**	Er **v**ro iwerzhoneger emaomp <u>bremañ</u>. **b>v**	Nous sommes <u>maintenant</u> au zone irlandophone.
Tha <u>muinntir an àite</u> càirdeil.	Tud a feson eo <u>tud ar **v**ro-mañ</u>. **b>v**	<u>Les gens du pays</u> sont sympas.

on the town
yn y dre
sa bhaile mhór
sa bhaile mhòr
e kêr
en ville

 english	 welsh cymraeg gallois	 irish gaeilge irlandais
To send a letter by air mail.	Anfon llythyr **d**rwy **b**ost awyr. t>d, p>b	Litir a **sh**eoladh san aerphost. s>sh
Excuse me. <u>I'm looking for</u> 1,070 X Street.	Esgusodwch fi. <u>Dwi'n chwilio am</u> 1,070 Stryd X.	Gabh mo leithscéal. <u>Tá mé ag lorg</u> 1,070 Sráid X.
<u>Go straight</u> and then take the second left.	<u>Cerwch yn syth</u> a **th**rowch i'r ail ar y chwith. t>th	<u>Gabh díreach romhat</u> agus lean an dara bóthar ar an láimh **ch**lé.
Sorry, <u>I don't know</u> where it is.	<u>Dwi **dd**im yn gwybod</u> ble mae e. Mae'n **dd**rwg gyda fi. d>dd, d>dd	<u>Níl a fhios agam</u> cáit a bhfuil sé. Tá brón orm. *níl=chan fhuil*
<u>You are going</u> in the wrong direction.	<u>Dych chi'n mynd</u> i'r cyfeiriad anghywir.	<u>Tá tú ag dul</u> ar seachrán/Tá amú ort.
Which is the shortest <u>way</u>?	Pa un yw'r <u>ffordd</u> **g**yflymaf? c>g	Cé an <u>bealach</u> is giorra?
It's <u>too far</u>!	Mae'n <u>rhy **b**ell</u>! p>b	Tá sé <u>ró-**fh**ada</u>! f>fh

 gaelic gàidhlig gaélique	 breton brezhoneg breton	français
Litir a **ch**ur sa **ph**ost adhar. c>ch, p>ph	Kas ul lizher **d**re **g**arr-nij. t>d, k>g	**Envoyer une lettre par avion.**
Gabh mo lethsgeul. <u>Tha mi a' lorg</u> 1,070 Sràid X.	Eskuzit ac'hanon. <u>Klask ran</u> 1070 Straed X.	**Excusez-moi. <u>Je cherche</u> 1070 Rue X.**
<u>Cum dìreach romhad</u> agus gabh an darna tionndadh ris an làimh **ch**lì. c>ch	<u>Kerzhit war-eeun</u> ha troit war an eil a **g**leiz. k>g	**<u>Allez tout droit</u>, puis prenez le deuxième à gauche.**
<u>Chan eil fhios agam</u> càit a bheil e. Tha mi duilich.	<u>Ne ouian ket</u> pelec'h emañ. Digarezit ac'hanon.	**Je regrette, <u>je ne sais pas</u>.**
<u>Tha sibh a' dol</u> air seachran/Tha sibh air seachran. <u>Tha sibh a' gabhail</u> an taoibh **ch**eàrr. c>ch	<u>Mont rit</u> a-dreuz.	**<u>Vouz allez</u> dans la mauvaise direction.**
Dè an <u>rathad</u> as giorra?	Peseurt <u>hent</u> eo an <u>hent</u> berrañ?	**Quel est le plus court <u>chemin</u>?**
Tha e <u>ro **fh**ada</u>! f>fh	<u>Re **b**ell</u> emañ! p>b	**C'est <u>trop loin</u>!**

121

 english	 welsh cymraeg gallois	irish gaeilge irlandais
Which is the best way to get <u>there</u>?	Beth yw'r ffordd **o**rau i **f**ynd <u>yna</u>? g>_, m>f	Cé **h-é** an dóigh is fearr le dul <u>ann</u>? é>h-é
You better go by <u>bus</u>.	Gyda'r <u>bws</u> **f**uasai'r ffordd **o**rau. b>f, g>_	Is é an <u>bus</u> an dóigh is fearr.
There's the <u>number</u> ten.	Dyna <u>rif</u> deg. rh>r	Sin <u>uimhir</u> a deich.
What is the name of <u>this street</u>?	Beth yw enw<u>'r stryd yma</u>?	Cén t-ainm atá ar <u>an **ts**ráid seo</u>? s>ts
I'm looking for <u>X Limited</u>.	Dwi'n chwilio am <u>X Cyfyngedig</u>.	Tá mé ag lorg <u>X Teoranta</u>.
Is there a <u>Mr John MacDonald</u> working here?	Oes <u>Mr John MacDonald</u> yn gweithio yma?	An bhfuil duine ar bith darb ainm <u>Seán Mac Dónaill</u> ag obair anseo?
I want to speak to X.	Dwi am **g**ael sgwrs gyda X. c>g	Ba **mh**aith liom comhrá a **dh**éanamh le X. m>mh, d>dh
Show me all the <u>interesting places</u>.	Dangos yr holl <u>lefydd diddorol</u> i fi. ll>l	Taispeáin na **h-á**iteanna <u>suimiúla</u> uile domh. á>h-á

 gaelic **gàidhlig** gaélique	 breton **brezhoneg** breton	🍷 français
Dè an dòigh as fheàrr airson dol <u>ann</u>?	Peseurt mod eo ar gwellañ da **v**ont <u>eno</u>? m>v	**Quel est le meilleur chemin pour s'<u>y</u> rendre?**
Is e am <u>bus</u> an dòigh as fheàrr.	E <u>karr-boutin</u> eo an tu gwellañ.	**Vous feriez mieux de prendre l'<u>autobus</u>.**
Sin <u>àireamh</u> a deich.	Setu <u>niverenn</u> dek.	**Voilà le <u>numéro</u> dix/Voilà le dix.**
Dè an t-ainm a tha air <u>an **t-s**ràid seo</u>? s>t-s	Peseurt anv zo gant <u>ar straed-mañ</u>?	**Quel est le nom de <u>cette rue</u>?**
Tha mi a' lorg <u>X Earranta</u>.	Klask rañ <u>X Bevennet</u>.	**Je cherche <u>X Limitée</u>.**
A' bheil duine sam bith don ainm <u>Seonaidh Mac Dhòmhnaill</u> ag obair an seo?	Bez eus un <u>Aotrou John MacDonald</u> o labourat amañ?	**Est-ce qu'il y a un <u>Mr John MacDonald</u> ici?**
Bu toil leam còmhradh a **dh**èanamh ri X.	Plijout a rafe din komz gant X.	**Je voudrais parler avec X.**
Seall na **h-à**itean inntinneach uile dhomh. à>h-à	Diskouez an holl <u>lec'hioù dedennus</u> din.	**Montrez-moi tous les <u>endroits intéressants</u>.**

 english	welsh cymraeg gallois	irish gaeilge irlandais
I prefer walking around <u>by myself</u>.	Mae'n **w**ell gyda fi **g**rwydro <u>ar fy **mh**en fy hun</u>. g>_, c>g, p>mh	B'**fh**earr liom a bheith ag siúl <u>i m'aonar</u>. f>fh
I'm going in to town <u>to see X</u>.	Dwi'n mynd i'r **d**re <u>i **w**eld X</u>. t>d, g>_	Tá mé ag dul go dtí an baile mór chun <u>X a **fh**eicsint</u>. f>fh
1. <u>Would you like</u> to come? *"you" singular familiar/ singulier familier*	1. <u>Am **dd**od</u>? d>dd	1. <u>Ar **mh**aith leat</u> teacht? m>mh
2. (Yes,) with pleasure.	2. Ydw, yn llawen/Ydw, ar **b**ob cyfrif/Ydw, â **ph**leser p>b, p>ph	2. Ba **mh**aith, cinnte. m>mh
2. <u>No</u>, thanks.	2. <u>Nac ydw</u>, diolch.	2. <u>Níor **mh**aith</u>, go raibh maith agat. m>mh, *níor=char*
1. What are <u>you</u> doing tonight? *plural/pluriel*	1. **B**eth dych <u>chi</u>'n **w**neud heno? *plural/pluriel g>_*	1. Goidé atá <u>sibh</u> ag déanamh anocht? *plural/pluriel*
1. *What are <u>you</u> doing tonight? singular/singulier*	1. Beth wyt <u>ti</u>'n **w**neud heno? *singular/singulier g>_*	1. Goidé atá <u>tú</u> ag déanamh anocht? *singular/singulier*

 gaelic **gàidhlig** gaélique	breton **brezhoneg** breton	français
B'**fhe**àrr leam dol mun cuairt 'n**am** aonar. f>fh	Gwelloc'h e vefe ganin bale <u>ma</u> unan-penn.	**Je préfère faire une promenade <u>tout seul</u>.**
Tha mi dol don **bh**aile **mh**òr gus X **fh**aicinn. b>bh, m>mh, f>fh	Mont a ran e kêr <u>da **w**elet</u> X. g>_	**Je m'en vais en ville <u>pour voir</u> X.**
1. <u>Am bu toil leat</u> tighinn?	1. <u>C'hoant ac'h eus</u> da **z**ont? d>z	**1. <u>Tu voudrais</u> m'accompagner?**
2. Bu toil, cinnteach.	2. Ya, laouen.	**2. (Oui,) avec plaisir.**
2. <u>Cha bu toil</u>, tapadh leat.	2. <u>Ne 'm eus ket</u>, trugarez.	**2. <u>Non</u>, merci.**
1. Dè tha <u>sibh</u> a' dèanamh a-nochd? *plural/pluriel*	1. Petra <u>rit</u> fenoz? *plural/pluriel*	**1. Qu'est-ce que <u>vous</u> allez faire ce soir?** *plural/pluriel*
1. Dè tha <u>thu</u> a' dèanamh a-nochd? *singular/singulier*	1. Petra rez fenoz? *singular/singulier*	**1. Qu'est-ce que <u>tu</u> va faire ce soir?** *singular/singulier*

 english	 welsh cymraeg gallois	irish gaeilge irlandais
2. i'm busy.	2. Dwi'n **b**rysur. p>b	2. Tá go leor rudaí le déanamh agam.
2. Nothing.	2. Dim byd.	2. Dada.
I want to go <u>to a nightclub</u>.	Dwi am **f**ynd i **gl**wb nos. m>f, c>g	Ba **mh**aith liomsa dul <u>go club oíche</u>. m>mh
There will be a lot <u>of people</u> in town on Saturday night.	Bydd llawer **o b**obl yn y **d**re nos Sadwrn. p>b, t>d	Beidh go leor <u>daoine</u> sa **bh**aile (**mh**ór) oíche **Sh**athairn. b>bh, m>mh, S>Sh
Peter is <u>drunk</u> in the tavern.	Mae Pedr **yn f**eddw yn y **d**afarn. m>f, t>d	Tá Peadar <u>ar meisce</u> sa teach tábhairne.
The music is <u>very loud</u> here.	Mae'r **g**erddoriaeth yn <u>uchel iawn</u> yma. c>g	Tá an ceol <u>an-ard</u> anseo.
<u>How much</u> does this cost?	**F**aint mae hwn yn costi? *(=pa + maint)*, **M>F**	<u>Cé **mh**éad</u> atá ar seo? m>mh
X is the <u>better</u> of the two. =*mieux*	X yw'r <u>gorau</u> o'r **dd**au. =*best/meilleur* d>dd	(Is é) X an ceann <u>is fearr</u> dhíobh. =*best/meilleur*

126

gaelic **gàidhlig** gaélique	breton **brezhoneg** breton	français
2. Tha gu leòr rudan ri **dh**èanamh agam. **d>dh**	2. Kalz traoù 'meus d'ober.	2. Je suis occupé(e)/J'ai beaucoup à faire.
2. Dad.	2. Netra/Mann bet.	2. Rien.
Bu toil leamsa dol <u>gu club oidhche</u>.	Plijout a rafe diñ mont <u>d'ur **v**oest noz</u>. **b>v**	Je veux aller <u>à une boîte de nuit</u>.
Bidh gu leòr a **dh**aoine sa **bh**aile (**mh**òr) oidhche Disathairne. **d>dh, b>bh, m>mh**	Ur bern <u>tud</u> vo e kêr disadorn d'an noz.	Il y aura beaucoup <u>de monde</u> en ville samedi soir.
Tha Peadar <u>air **mh**isge</u> anns an taigh-òsda. **m>mh**	Per zo <u>mezv</u> en **d**avarn. **t>d**	Pierre est <u>bourré</u> au bar.
Tha an ceòl <u>glè àrd</u> an seo.	Ar sonerezh zo <u>kreñv-mat</u> amañ.	La musique est <u>très forte</u> ici.
Dè na a tha air seo?	<u>Pegement</u> a **g**oust an **d**ra-mañ? **k>g, t>d**	<u>Combien</u> est-ce qu'il coûte celui-là?
(Is e) X am fear <u>as fheàrr</u> dhiùbh. =*best/meilleur*	X eo ar <u>gwellañ</u> eus an daou. =*best/meilleur*	C'est X le <u>meilleur</u> des deux. =*best*

english

 welsh **cymraeg** gallois

 irish **gaeilge** irlandais

english	welsh cymraeg gallois	irish gaeilge irlandais
Do you speak <u>French</u>? yes	Ydych chi'n siarad <u>Ffrangeg</u>? ydw	An bhfuil <u>an **Fh**raincis</u> agaibh? tá
Do you speak <u>Irish</u>? no	Wyt ti'n siarad <u>Gwyddeleg</u>? nac ydw (na)	An bhfuil <u>an **Gh**aeilge</u> agat? **G>Gh** níl (chan fhuil)
We will see you <u>tomorrow</u>.	Gwelwn ni chi <u>fory</u>/Gwnawn ni eich gweld <u>fory</u>.	Chífidh muid <u>amáireach</u> sibh.
It is not <u>far</u> from here.	Dyw e **dd**im yn **b**ell o 'ma. **d>dd**, **p>b**	Níl sé <u>fada</u> ón áit seo Chan fhuil sé <u>fada</u> ón áit seo.

gaelic **gàidhlig** gaélique	breton **brezhoneg** breton	français

A bheil an **Fh**raingis agaibh?
  tha
	C'hwi oar galleg?
	  ya
		Parlez-vous français?
		  oui

A bheil Gàidhlig na **h-È**ireann agad? È>h-È
  chan eil
	Te oar iwerzhoneg?
	
	  ne ouian ket
		Est-ce que tu parle irlandais?
		
		  non

Chì sinn a-màireach sibh.	Benn warc'hoazh.	**À demain.**
Chan eil e fad' as.	N'emañ ket pell eus al lec'h-mañ.	**C'est pas loin d'ici.**

money
arian
airgead
airgead
arc'hant
argent

 english	 welsh cymraeg gallois	irish gaeilge irlandais
We don't have a lot <u>of cash</u>.	Does dim llawer <u>o arian parod</u> gyda ni.	Níl mórán <u>airgid</u> againn/Chan fhuil mórán <u>airgid</u> againn.
Do you accept <u>Visa credit cards</u> here?	A ydych chi'n derbyn <u>cardiau credyd Visa</u>?	An **ng**lacann sibh le <u>cártaí creidmheasa Visa</u> anseo? g>ng

Is the bank <u>open</u>?
    yes
    no
	Ydi'r banc <u>ar agor</u>?
	    ydi
	    nac ydi (na)
		An bhfuil an banc <u>foscailte</u>?
		    tá
		    níl (chan fhuil) = _ar oscailt_

I would like £200 (two hundred pounds) in <u>traveller's cheques</u>.	Dwi eisiau £200 (dau **g**an punt) o <u>sieciau teithio</u> os gwelwch yn **dd**a. c>g, d>dd	Ba **mh**aith liom £200 (dhá **ch**éad punt) de <u>**sh**eiceanna taistil</u> más é do **th**oil é. m>mh, c>ch, s>sh, t>th
The English <u>pound</u>	Y **b**unt Seisnig p>b	An <u>punt</u> Sasanach
The <u>Scottish</u> pound	Y **b**unt <u>Albanaidd</u> p>b	An punt <u>Albanach</u>

 gaelic **gàidhlig** gaélique	 breton **brezhoneg** breton	français
Chan eil mórán airgid againn.	N'eus ket kalz arc'hant ganeomp.	**Nous n'avons pas beaucoup de liquide.**
An gabh sibh cairtean creideas Visa an seo?	Degemeret **v**ez kartennoù kredit Visa amañ? **b>v**	**Acceptez-vous les cartes de crédit Visa ici?**
A bheil am banc fosgailte? tha chan eil	Digoret eo an ti-bank? ya n'eo ket	**Est-ce que la banque est ouverte?** oui non
Bu toil leam £200 (dà **ch**eud not) de **sh**eicean taisdil mas e'r toil e. **c>ch, s>sh**	C'hoant am eus da **g**aout £200 (daou **g**ant lur saoz) e chekoù beajiñ mar plij. **k>g, k>g**	**Je voudrais £200 (deux cent livres) en chèques de voyages s'il vous plaît.**
Am punnd Sasannach	Al lur saoz	**La livre anglais**
Am punnd Albannach	Al lur skos	**La livre écossaise**

133

exploring
anturio
taiscéaladh
sùil mun cuairt
klask dizolo
à la découverte

 english	 welsh cymraeg gallois	irish gaeilge irlandais
I prefer Galway to Limerick.	Mae'n well gyda fi Galway na Limerick. g>_	Is fearr liom Gaillimh ná Luimneach.
Fishing is important on the Isle of Lewis.	Mae'r pysgota yn bwysig yn Ynys Lewis. p>b	Is tábhachtach an t-iascach/an iascaireacht i Leòdhas. i>t-i
There is a new bridge to the Isle of Skye.	Mae pont newydd i Ynys Sgiathanach.	Tá droichead úr don Oileán Sgiathanach. úr=nua
We were in Inishmore in the Aran Islands yesterday.	Buon ni yn Inis Mór yn Ynysoedd Árann ddoe.	Bhí muid in Inis Mór Árann inné.
It is in the West of Brittany that they speak Breton.	Yn Llydaw Isaf y mae'r Llydaweg.	I mBriotáin Íochtar atá an Bhriotánais. B>mB, B>Bh
Most of the coal mines of Wales are closed.	Mae'r rhan fwya o byllau glo Cymru wedi cau. m>f, p>b	Tá an chuid is mó de mhianaigh ghuail na Breataine Bige i ndiaidh dúnaidh. c>ch, m>mh, g>gh, d>nd
Is there an underground in Carmarthen? No, stupid!	Oes trên tanddaearol yng Nghaerfyrddin? Nac oes, y twpsyn! C>Ngh	An bhfuil traen faoi thalamh i gCaerfyrddin? Níl (Chan fhuil), amadáin! t>th, C>gC

gaelic **gàidhlig** gaélique	breton **brezhoneg** breton	🍷 français
<u>Is fheàrr leam</u> Gaillimh na Luimneach.	<u>Gwelloc'h eo ganin</u> Galway eget Limerick.	**<u>Je préfère</u> Galway à Limerick.**
Tha **an t-i**asgach cudthromach ann an Leòdhas. **i>t-i**	Ar **p**esketaerezh zo a **b**ouez en enez Leòdhas. **p>b**	**<u>La pêche</u> est importante dans l'Île de Lewis.**
Tha <u>drochaid ùr</u> don Eilean Sgiathanach.	<u>Ur pont nevez</u> zo evit mont d'an Enez Sgiathanach.	**Il y a <u>un nouveau pont</u> pour aller à l'Île de Skye.**
Bha sinn an Inis Mór Árann <u>an-dè</u>.	Bez e oamp en Inis Mór Árann <u>dec'h</u>.	**On était sur l'Inishmore aux Îles d'Aran <u>hier</u>.**
Is ann an Ìochdar na Breatainn Bige a tha **a' Bh**reatannais. **B>Bh**	E Breiz Izel emañ <u>ar brezhoneg</u>.	**C'est en Basse-Bretagne qu'on parle <u>le breton</u>.**
Tha a' **ch**uid as motha de **mh**èinntean guail **na** Cuimrigh an dèidh dùnaidh. **c>ch, m>mh**	Serret eo al lodenn **v**rasañ eus mengleuzioù glaou <u>Kembre</u>. **b>v**	**Le plupart des mines de charbon <u>du Pays de Galles</u> sont fermées.**
A bheil <u>trèan fon talamh</u> ann an Carmarthen? Chan eil, amadain!	Bez ez eus <u>ur metro</u> e Carmarthen? N'eus ket, genaouek!	**Est-ce qu'il y a <u>un métro</u> à Carmarthen? Mais non, imbécile!**

culture and entertainment
diwylliant ac adloniant
cultúr is siamsa
cultar is cuirm
sevenadur ha diduamant
culture et divertissement

 english	 welsh cymraeg gallois	 irish gaeilge irlandais
The Pan-Celtic Festival	Yr Ŵyl Ban-Geltaidd G>_, P>B, C>G	An Fhéile Phan-Cheilteach F>Fh, P>Ph, C>Ch
Let's go see the Irish-language T.V. station in Connemara.	Awn ni i weld gorsaf y teledu Gwyddeleg yn Conamara. g>_ (yng Nghonamara)	Gabhaimid go Stáisiún Theilifís na Gaeilge i gConamara. T>Th, C>gC
Breton music	Cerddoriaeth Llydaw	Ceol na Briotáine
What is the Breton word for X?	Beth yw'r Llydaweg am X? = pa + peth	Cé an Bhriotánais atá ar X? B>Bh
There is a Gaelic programme on T.V. at five-thirty.	Mae rhaglen Aeleg ar y teledu am hanner awr wedi pump. G>_	Tá clár Gaeilge na h-Alban ar an teilifís ar leath-uair i ndiaidh a cúig. A>h-A, d>nd
There is a cèilidh tonight at 7:00.	Bydd cèilidh heno am 7:00.	Beidh céilí anocht ar a 7:00.
There are approximately a thousand Welsh-speakers in Argentina.	Mae tua mil o bobl yr Ariannin yn siarad Cymraeg	Tá an Bhreatnais ag timpeall míle duine san Airgintín. B>Bh

gaelic gàidhlig gaélique	breton brezhoneg breton	français
An **Fhè**ile **Ph**an-**Ch**eilteach F>Fh, P>Ph, C>Ch	<u>Ar gouel</u> oll-**g**eltiek k>g	<u>Le festival</u> inter-celtique
Nach tèid sinn gu Stèisean Teilifís na Gaeilge <u>ann an Conamara</u>.	Deomp da studioioù Tele an iwerzhoneg <u>e Konamara</u>.	Allons aux studios de télé en langue irlandaise <u>dans le Connemara</u>.
Ceòl na Breatainne Bige	Sonerez Breizh	La musique bretonne
<u>Dè</u> a' **Bh**reatannais a tha air X? B>Bh	<u>Petra</u> eo ar brezhoneg evit X?	<u>Quel</u> est le mot breton pour X?
Tha prògram Gàidhlig air an T.V. <u>aig leth-uair an dèidh a còig</u>.	Un abadenn **o**uezeleg zo b'an tele **d**a **b**embeur hanter. g>_, p>b	Il y a une émission gaélique à la télé <u>à cinq heures et demie</u>.
Bidh cèilidh <u>a-nochd</u> aig a 7:00.	Ur c'hèilidh vo da 7:00 <u>fenoz</u>.	Il y aura un cèilidh <u>ce soir</u> à 7:00. *7:00 soir = 19:00 h*
Tha a' **Ch**uimris aig timcheall <u>mìle</u> duine ann an Argentina. C>Ch	War-**d**ro <u>ur mil</u> den en Arc'hantina a oar kembraeg. t>d	Il y a environ <u>un millier</u> de personnes qui parlent le gallois en Argentine.

141

 english	 welsh cymraeg gallois	irish gaeilge irlandais
What is <u>on T.V.</u> at ten (o'clock)?	**B**eth sy <u>ar y teledu</u> am **dd**eg (o'r gloch)? = *pa + peth*, **d>dd**	Goidé atá <u>ar an teilifís</u> ar a deich (a chlog)? *cé=céard=cén rud=cad é=goidé=dé*
The museum is in the <u>centre of town</u>.	Yng **ngh**anol y **d**re y mae'r amgueddfa. **c>ngh, t>d**	I <u>lár an **bh**aile</u> atá an iarsmalann. **b>bh**
It is worth seeing Sain Ffagan's <u>Museum</u> (Cardiff).	Mae <u>Amgueddfa</u> Sain Ffagan (Caerdydd) yn **w**erth ei gweld. **g>_**	Is fiú <u>Iarsmalann</u> **Sh**ain Ffagan (Caerdydd) a **fh**eicsint. **S>Sh, f>fh**
We want to try some of the local <u>cuisine</u>.	Dyn ni am **g**ael blas ar **g**oginio'r **f**ro yma. **c>g, c>g, b>f**	Ba **mh**aith linn blas ar <u>**bh**ia</u> an **ch**eantair a **fh**áil. **m>mh, b>bh, c>ch, f>fh**
What <u>films</u> are playing at the cinema?	Pa <u>ff**ilmiau</u> sy yn y sinema?	Cé **h-i**ad na <u>scannáin</u> atá sa **ph**ictiúrlann? **i>h-i, p>ph**
The Eisteddfod is in the first week <u>of August</u>.	Mae'r Eisteddfod yn wythnos **g**ynta <u>Awst</u>. **c>g**	Sa **ch**éad seachtain <u>de **mh**í Lúnasa</u> a **bh**íonn an Eisteddfod. **c>ch, m>mh, b>bh**
There will be a fest-noz <u>next week</u> in Spézet.	Bydd fest-noz <u>yr wythnos nesa</u> yn Spezed.	Beidh fest-noz <u>an **t-s**eachtain seo chugainn</u> i Spezed. **s>t-s**

142

 gaelic **gàidhlig** gaélique	breton **brezhoneg** breton	français
Dè tha <u>air an T.V.</u> aig a deich (aig deich uairean)? *cia=dè (an) rud=ciod e=gu dè=dè*	Petra zo <u>en tele</u> da **z**ek eur? **d>z**	Qu'est-ce qu'il y a <u>à la télé</u> à dix heures?
Is ann am <u>meadhan a' **bh**aile</u> a tha an taigh-tasgaidh. **b>bh**	E <u>kreiz-kêr</u> emañ ar mirdi.	C'est au <u>centre-ville</u> que se trouve le musée.
Is fiù <u>Taigh-Tasgaidh **Sh**ain</u> Ffagan (Caerdydd) a **fh**aicinn. **S>Sh, f>fh**	<u>Mirdi</u> Sain Ffagan (Caerdydd) a **d**alvez bezañ gwelet. **t>d**	Ça vaut la peine de voir le <u>musée</u> de Sain Ffagan (Cardiff).
Bu toil leinn blas <u>biadh</u> an àite seo a **fh**euchainn. **f>fh**	C'hoant hon eus da **d**añva <u>keginerezh</u> ar **v**ro-mañ. **t>d, b>v**	Nous voudrions goûter la <u>cuisine</u> locale.
Dè na <u>filmichean</u> a tha san taigh-**dh**ealbh? **d>dh**	Peseurt <u>filmoù</u> zo er sinema?	Qu'est-ce qu'il y a au cinéma comme <u>films</u>?
Is ann sa **ch**eud sheachdain <u>den Lùnasdal</u> a **bh**ios an Eisteddfod. **c>ch, s>sh, b>bh**	E sizhun kentañ <u>miz eost</u> e **v**ez an Eisteddfod. **b>v**	L'Eisteddfod est pendant la première semaine <u>d'août</u>.
Bidh fest-noz <u>an ath-**sh**eachdain</u> ann an Spezed. **s>sh**	Ur fest-noz a vo e Spezed <u>ar sizhun a **z**eu.</u> **d>z**	Il y aura un fest-noz à Spézet <u>la semaine prochaine</u>.

english	welsh cymraeg gallois	irish gaeilge irlandais
There are around 70,000 Gaelic speakers in Scotland.	Mae tua <u>saith deg mil</u> o **b**obl yr Alban yn siarad Gaeleg. p>b =_deg a thrigain mil_	Tá Gaeilge na **h-A**lban ag timpeall <u>trí scór is deich míle</u> duine in Albain. A>h-A

144

 gaelic **gàidhlig** gaélique	 breton **brezhoneg** breton	français
Tha a' **Gh**àidhlig aig timcheall <u>trì fichead 's a deich mìle</u> duine ann an Albainn. **G>Gh**	War-**d**ro <u>dek ha tri-ugent mil</u> den e Bro-Skos a oar gouezeleg. **t>d**	Il y a à peu près <u>soixante-dix mille</u> de personnes en Écosse qui parlent le gaélique.

some proverbs
diarhebion
sean-fhocail
sean-fhacail
krennlavarioù
des proverbes

welsh
cymraeg gallois

irish
gaeilge irlandais

"HANNER Y DAITH <u>CYCHWYN</u>"
Half the trip is <u>starting</u> out
La moitié du voyage, c'est le <u>départ</u>

"GO N-ÉIRÍ <u>AN BÓTHAR</u> LEAT"
May <u>the road</u> rise to meet you = Good luck on the journey
Que <u>la route</u> se lève pour toi = Bonne route

gaelic
gàidhlig gaélique

"IS E OBAIR LÀ TÒISEACHADH"

Starting is a day's work
Commencer, c'est le travail d'une journée

"CHA DO DHÙIN DORAS NACH D' FHOSGAIL DORAS"

A door didn't shut that a door didn't open
Aucune porte n'est fermée sans qu'une autre n'est ouverte

"DÀ IOLAIR AIR IODHLANN IOLAIR FHIREANN 'S IOLAIR BHOIREANN"

Two eagles on a fence (cornyard) – a male and a female
Deux aigles sur une clôture – un mâle et une femelle

breton
brezhoneg breton

"SKLAER VEL LAGAD UN NAER"

Clear like the eye of a snake
Clair comme l' oeil d'un serpent

numbers
rhifau
uimhreacha
àireamhan
niverennoù
numéros

english	 welsh cymraeg gallois	irish gaeilge irlandais
1 one	1 un	1 aon
2 two	2 dau (dwy)	2 dhá/dá
3 three	3 tri (tair)	3 trí
4 four	4 pedwar (pedair)	4 ceithre
5 five	5 pump	5 cúig
6 six	6 chwech	6 sé
7 seven	7 saith	7 seacht
8 eight	8 wyth	8 ocht
9 nine	9 naw	9 naoi
10 ten	10 deg	10 deich
11 eleven	11 un ar ddeg/un deg un	11 aon déag
12 twelve	12 deuddeg/un deg dau	12 dhá dhéag
13 thirteen	13 tri (tair) ar ddeg/ un deg tri	13 trí déag
14 fourteen	14 pedwar (pedair) ar ddeg/ un deg pedwar	14 ceithre déag
15 fifteen	15 pymtheg/un deg pump	15 cúig déag
16 sixteen	16 un ar bymtheg/ un deg chwech	16 sé déag
17 seventeen	17 dau (dwy) ar bymtheg/ un deg saith	17 seacht déag
18 eighteen	18 deunaw/un deg wyth	18 ocht déag
19 nineteen	19 pedwar (pedair) ar bymtheg/un deg naw	19 naoi déag
20 twenty	20 ugain	20 fiche/fichead/fichid

gaelic gàidhlig gaélique	breton brezhoneg breton	français
1 aon	1 unan	1 un *(une)*
2 dà	2 daou *(div)*	2 deux
3 trì	3 tri *(teir)*	3 trois
4 ceithir	4 pevar *(peder)*	4 quatre
5 còig	5 pemp	5 cinq
6 sia / sè	6 c'hwec'h	6 six
7 seachd	7 seizh	7 sept
8 ochd	8 eizh	8 huit
9 naoi	9 nav	9 neuf
10 deich	10 dek	10 dix
11 aon deug	11 unnek	11 onze
12 dà dheug	12 daouzek	12 douze
13 trì deug	13 trizek	13 treize
14 ceithir deug	14 pevarzek	14 quatorze
15 còig deug	15 pemzek	15 quinze
16 sia deug / sè deug	16 c'hwezek	16 seize
17 seachd deug	17 seitek	17 dix-sept
18 ochd deug	18 triwec'h	18 dix-huit
19 naoi deug	19 naontek	19 dix-neuf
20 fichead	20 ugent	20 vingt

 english	 welsh cymraeg gallois	 irish gaeilge irlandais
80 eighty	80 pedwar ugain/wyth deg	80 ceithre fichid/ochtó
99 ninety-nine	99 cant namyn un/ naw deg naw	99 naoi déag is ceithre fichid/ nócha naoi
100 one hundred	100 cant	100 céad
150 one hundred and fifty	150 cant a hanner	150 caoga agus céad
1000 one thousand	1000 mil	1000 míle

Counting / Compter

1 a haon
2 a dó
3 a trí
4 a ceathair
5 a cúig
6 a sé
7 a seacht
8 a h-ocht
9 a naoi
10 a deich
11 a haon déag
12 a dó dhéag
13 a trí déag
14 a ceathair déag
15 a cúig déag
16 a sé déag
17 a seacht déag
18 a hocht déag
19 a naoi déag
20 a fiche/a fichead

gaelic
gàidhlig gaélique

breton
brezhoneg breton

français

gaelic gàidhlig gaélique	breton brezhoneg breton	français
80 ceithir fichead/ochdad	80 pevar ugent	**80 quatre-vingts**
99 ceithir fichead 's a naoi deug	99 kant nemet unan	**99 quatre-vingts dix-neuf**
100 ceud	100 kant	**100 cent**
150 ceud gu leth	150 ur c'hant hanter / kant hanter kant	**150 cent cinquante**
1000 mìle	1000 mil	**1000 mille**

Counting / Compter

1 a h-aon
2 a dhà
3 a trì
4 a ceithir
5 a còig
6 a sia / a sè
7 a seachd
8 a h-ochd
9 a naoi
10 a deich
11 a h-aon deug
12 a dhà dheug
13 a trì deug
14 a ceithir deug
15 a còig deug
16 a sia deug / a sè deug
17 a seachd deug
18 a h-ochd deug
19 a naoi deug
20 a fichead

155

time
yr <u>amser</u>
an t-<u>am</u>
an t-<u>àm</u>
an <u>amzer</u>
le <u>temps</u>

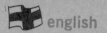 english	 welsh cymraeg gallois	 irish gaeilge irlandais
DAYS OF THE WEEK	DYDDIAU'R WYTHNOS	LAETHANTA NA SEACHTAINE

	english		welsh		irish
1	Monday	1	dydd Llun	Llun	1	an Luan
2	Tuesday	2	dydd Mawrth	Mawrth	2	an Mháirt
3	Wednesday	3	dydd Mercher	Mercher	3	an Chéadaoin
4	Thursday	4	dydd Iau	Iau	4	an Déardaoin
5	Friday	5	dydd Gwener	Gwener	5	an Aoine
6	Saturday	6	dydd Sadwrn	Sadwrn	6	an Satharn
7	Sunday	7	dydd Sul	Sul	7	an Domhnach

HABITUAL

	english		welsh		irish
1	on Mondays	1	ar ddydd Llun	1	ar an Luan
2	on Tuesdays	2	ar ddydd Mawrth	2	ar an **Mh**áirt/ar an Máirt
3	on Wednesdays	3	ar ddydd Mercher	3	ar an **Ch**éadaoin/ar an **gC**éadaoin
4	on Thursdays	4	ar ddydd Iau	4	ar an Déardaoin
5	on Fridays	5	ar ddydd Gwener	5	ar an Aoine
6	on Saturdays	6	ar ddydd Sadwrn	6	ar an **t-S**atharn/ar an Satharn
7	on Sundays	7	ar ddydd Sul/ar y Sul	7	ar an Domhnach

 gaelic **gàidhlig** gaélique	 breton **brezhoneg** breton	français
LÀITHEAN NA SEACHDAIN	DEIZIOÙ AR SIZHUN	LES JOURS DE LA SEMAINE

gaelic	breton		français
1 Diluain	1 dilun	al Lun	1 lundi
2 Dimàirt	2 dimeurzh	ar Meurzh	2 mardi
3 Diciadain	3 dimerc'her	ar Merc'her	3 mercredi
4 Diardaoin	4 diriaou	ar Yaou	4 jeudi
5 Dihaoine	5 digwener	ar Gwener	5 vendredi
6 Disathairne	6 disadorn	ar Sadorn	6 samedi
7 Didòmhnaich/Là na Sàbaid	7 disul	ar Sul	7 dimanche

HABITUAL (français)

gaelic	breton	français
1 Diluain	1 d'al Lun	1 le/les lundi (s)
2 Dimàirt	2 d'ar Meurzh	2 le/les mardi (s)
3 Diciadain	3 d'ar Merc'her	3 le/les mercredi (s)
4 Diardaoin	4 d'ar Yaou	4 le/les jeudi (s)
5 Dihaoine	5 d'ar Gwener	5 le/les vendredi (s)
6 Disathairne	6 d'ar Sadorn	6 le/les samedi (s)
7 Didòmhnaich/Là na Sàbaid	7 d'ar Sul	7 le/les dimanche (s)

 english	welsh **cymraeg** gallois	irish **gaeilge** irlandais
PAST.FUTURE		
1 on/this Monday	1 ddydd Llun	1 Dé Luain
2 on/this Tuesday	2 ddydd Mawrth	2 Dé Máirt
3 on/this Wednesday	3 ddydd Mercher	3 Dé Céadaoin
4 on/this Thursday	4 ddydd Iau	4 Déardaoin
5 on/this Friday	5 ddydd Gwener	5 Dé hAoine
6 on/this Saturday	6 ddydd Sadwrn	6 Dé Sathairn
7 on/this Sunday	7 ddydd Sul	7 Dé Domhnaigh
THE <u>MONTHS</u>	Y <u>MISOEDD</u>	NA <u>MÍONNA</u>
1 January	1 (mis) Ionawr	1 mí Eanáir
2 February	2 (mis) Chwefror	2 mí Feabhra
3 March	3 (mis) Mawrth	3 mí an Mhárta
4 April	4 (mis) Ebrill	4 mí Aibreáin
5 May	5 (mis) Mai	5 an Bhealtaine
6 June	6 (mis) Mehefin	6 Meitheamh
7 July	7 (mis) Gorffennaf	7 mí Iúil
8 August	8 (mis) Awst	8 mí Lúnasa
9 September	9 (mis) Medi	9 Meán Fómhair
10 October	10 (mis) Hydref	10 Deireadh Fómhair
11 November	11 (mis) Tachwedd	11 mí na Samhna/Samhain
12 December	12 (mis) Rhagfyr	12 mí na Nollag

gaelic
gàidhlig gaélique

1 Diluain
2 Dimàirt
3 Diciadaoin
4 Diardaoin
5 Dihaoine
6 Disathairne
7 Didòmhnaich/Là na Sàbaid

NA <u>MÌOSAN</u>
  1 Am Faoilleach
  2 An Gearran
  3 Am Màrt
  4 An Giblean
  5 An Cèitean/a' Mhàigh
  6 An t-Òg-Mhios
  7 An t-Iuchar
  8 An Lùnasdal
  9 An t-Sultain
10 An Damhair
11 An t-Samhain
12 An Dùbhlachd

breton
brezhoneg breton

1 dilun   (benn) dilun
2 dimeurzh   (benn) dimeurzh
3 dimerc'her   (benn) dimerc'her
4 diraou   (benn) diraou
5 digwener   (benn) digwener
6 disadorn   (benn) disadorn
7 disul   (benn) disul
past/passé   *future/futur*

AR <u>MIZOÙ</u>
  1 (miz) Genver
  2 (miz) C'hwevrer
  3 (miz) Meurzh
  4 (miz) Ebrel
  5 (miz) Mae
  6 (miz) Mezheven
  7 (miz) Gouere
  8 (miz) Eost
  9 (miz) Gwengolo
10 (miz) Here
11 (miz) Du
12 (miz) Kerzu

français

PASSÉ, FUTUR
1 **lundi**
2 **mardi**
3 **mercredi**
4 **jeudi**
5 **vendredi**
6 **samedi**
7 **dimanche**

LES <u>MOIS</u>
  1 **janvier**
  2 **février**
  3 **mars**
  4 **avril**
  5 **mai**
  6 **juin**
  7 **juillet**
  8 **août**
  9 **septembre**
10 **octobre**
11 **novembre**
12 **décembre**

 english	 welsh cymraeg gallois	 irish gaeilge irlandais
GENERAL	CYFFREDINOL	GINEARÁLTA
today	heddiw	inniu
tomorrow	yfory	amáireach
yesterday	ddoe	inné
this week	yr wythnos yma	an t-seachtain seo
tonight	heno	anocht
tomorrow night	nos fory	oíche amáireach
last night	neithiwr	aréir
the morning	y bore	an mhaidin
midday	canol dydd	meán lae
the afternoon	y prynhawn	an tráthnóna
the evening	y noswaith	an tráthnóna
the night	y nos	an oíche
midnight	hanner nos	meán-oíche

 gaelic **gàidhlig** gaélique	 breton **brezhoneg** breton	français
SAN FHARSAINGEACHD	A-VRAS	**GÉNÉRALITÉS**
an-diugh	hiziv	**aujourd'hui**
a-màireach	warc'hoazh	**demain**
an-dè	dec'h	**hier**
an t-seachdain seo	ar sizhun-mañ	**cette semaine**
a-nochd	fenoz	**ce soir**
an ath-oidhch'	warc'hoazh d'an noz	**demain soir**
a-raoir	dec'h d'an noz	**hier soir**
a' mhadainn	ar mintin/ar beure	**le matin**
meadhan là	kreisteiz	**midi**
an tràth-nòin	goude lein/goude mern	**après-midi**
am feasgar	an endervez	**la soirée**
an oidhche	an abardaez	**le soir**
meadhan-oidhche	hanternoz	**minuit**

wyt ti
tá tú
tha thu
te zo

to be
bod
tá
tha
bezañ
être

 english			welsh cymraeg gallois		irish gaeilge irlandais	

PRESENT

3	X	is		3	mae X		3	tá X
1	I	am		1	dwi		1	tá mé
2	you	are		2	rwyt ti		2	tá tú
3	he	is		3	mae e		3	tá sé
3	she	is		3	mae hi		3	tá sí
1x	we	are		1x	dyn ni		1x	tá muid
2x	you	are		2x	dych chi		2x	tá sibh
3x	they	are		3x	maen nhw		3x	tá siad

3	X	is	not	3	dyw X	ddim	3	níl X*
1	I	am	not	1	dwi	ddim	1	níl mé
2	you	are	not	2	dwyt ti	ddim	2	níl tú
3	he	is	not	3	dyw e	ddim	3	níl sé
3	she	is	not	3	dyw hi	ddim	3	níl sí
1x	we	are	not	1x	dyn ni	ddim	1x	níl muid
2x	you	are	not	2x	dych chi	ddim	2x	níl sibh
3x	they	are	not	3x	dyn nhw	ddim	3x	níl siad

*= *chan fhuil X (Ulster)*

gaelic
gàidhlig gaélique

breton
brezhoneg breton

français

PRÉSENT

gaelic	breton	français
3 <u>tha X</u>	3 <u>X zo</u>	3 <u>X est</u>
1 tha mi	1 me zo	1 je suis
2 tha thu	2 te zo	2 tu es
3 tha e	3 eñ/hennezh zo	3 il est
3 tha i	3 hi/hounnezh zo	3 elle est
1x tha sinn	1x ni zo	1x nous sommes
2x tha sibh	2x c'hwi zo	2x vous êtes
3x tha iad	3x int zo/ar re-se zo	3x ils/elles sont

gaelic	breton		français
3 <u>chan eil X</u>	3 <u>X n'eo ket</u>[1]	<u>X n'emañ ket</u>[2]	3 <u>X n'est pas</u>
1 chan eil mi	1 n'on ket	n'emaon ket	1 je ne suis pas
2 chan eil thu	2 n'out ket	n'emaout ket	2 tu n'es pas
3 chan eil e	3 n'eo ket	n'emañ ket	3 il n'est pas
3 chan eil i	3 n'eo ket	n'emañ ket	3 elle n'est pas
1x chan eil sinn	1x n'omp ket	n'emaomp ket	1x nous ne sommes pas
2x chan eil sibh	2x n'oc'h ket	n'emaoc'h ket	2x vous n'êtes pas
3x chan eil iad	3x n'int ket	n'emaint ket	3x ils/elles ne sont pas

[1] *for describing/pour décrire*
[2] *for situating/pour situer*

english			welsh cymraeg gallois			irish gaeilge irlandais	

FUTURE

3	<u>X</u>	<u>will be</u>		3	<u>bydd X</u>			3	<u>beidh X</u>
1	I	will be		1	bydda i			1	beidh mé
2	you	will be		2	byddi di			2	beidh tú
3	he	will be		3	bydd e			3	beidh sé
3	she	will be		3	bydd hi			3	beidh sí
1x	we	will be		1x	byddwn ni			1x	beidh muid
2x	you	will be		2x	byddwch chi			2x	beidh sibh
3x	they	will be		3x	byddan nhw			3x	beidh siad
3	<u>X</u>	<u>will not be</u>		3	<u>fydd X</u>	<u>ddim</u>		3	<u>ní bheidh X*</u>
1	I	will not be		1	fydda i	ddim		1	ní bheidh mé
2	you	will not be		2	fyddi di	ddim		2	ní bheidh tú
3	he	will not be		3	fydd e	ddim		3	ní bheidh sé
3	she	will not be		3	fydd hi	ddim		3	ní bheidh sí
1x	we	will not be		1x	fyddwn ni	ddim		1x	ní bheidh muid
2x	you	will not be		2x	fyddwch chi	ddim		2x	ní bheidh sibh
3x	they	will not be		3x	fyddan nhw	ddim		3x	ní bheidh siad

= cha bheidh X (Ulster)

168

FUTUR

3	<u>bidh X</u>	3	<u>X vo</u>	3	<u>X sera</u>
1	bidh mi	1	me vo	1	je serai
2	bidh tu	2	te vo	2	tu seras
3	bidh e	3	eñ/hennezh vo	3	il sera
3	bidh i	3	hi/hounnezh vo	3	elle sera
1x	bidh sinn	1x	ni vo	1x	nous serons
2x	bidh sibh	2x	c'hwi vo	2x	vous serez
3x	bidh iad	3x	int vo/ar re-se vo	3x	ils/elles seront

3	<u>cha bhi X</u>	3	<u>X ne vo</u> <u>ket</u>	3	<u>X ne sera pas</u>
1	cha bhi mi	1	ne vin ket	1	je ne serai pas
2	cha bhi thu	2	ne vi ket	2	tu ne seras pas
3	cha bhi e	3	ne vo ket	3	il ne sera pas
3	cha bhi i	3	ne vo ket	3	elle ne sera pas
1x	cha bhi sinn	1x	ne vimp ket	1x	nous ne serons pas
2x	cha bhi sibh	2x	ne viot ket	2x	vous ne serez pas
3x	cha bhi iad	3x	ne vint ket	3x	ils/elles ne seront pas

 english			 welsh cymraeg gallois		 irish gaeilge irlandais	
PRESENT QUESTION						
3	<u>Is</u>	<u>X?</u>	3	<u>ydi X?</u>	3	<u>an bhfuil X?</u>
1	am	I?	1	ydw i?	1	an bhfuil mé?
2	are	you?	2	wyt ti?	2	an bhfuil tú?
3	is	he?	3	ydi e?	3	an bhfuil sé?
3	is	she?	3	ydi hi?	3	an bhfuil sí?
1x	are	we?	1x	ydyn ni?	1x	an bhfuil muid?
2x	are	you?	2x	ydych chi?	2x	an bhfuil sibh?
3x	are	they?	3x	ydyn nhw?	3x	an bhfuil siad?
3	<u>yes</u>	<u>no</u>	3	<u>ydi</u>	<u>nac ydi/nac yw (na)</u>	3	<u>tá</u>	<u>níl</u>
1	yes	no	1	ydw	nac ydw (na)	1	tá	níl
2	yes	no	2	wyt	nac wyt (na)	2	tá	níl
3	yes	no	3	ydi	nac ydi/nac yw (na)	3	tá	níl
3	yes	no	3	ydi	nac ydi/nac yw (na)	3	tá	níl
1x	yes	no	1x	ydyn	nac ydyn (na)	1x	tá	níl
2x	yes	no	2x	ydych	nac ydych (na)	2x	tá	níl
3x	yes	no	3x	ydyn	nac ydyn (na)	3x	tá	níl

 gaelic **gàidhlig** gaélique	 breton **brezhoneg** breton	français

PRÉSENT QUESTION

	gaelic			breton			français	
3	<u>a bheil X?</u>		3	<u>X zo?</u>		3	<u>est-ce que X est?</u>	
1	a bheil mi?		1	me zo?		1	est-ce que je suis?	
2	a bheil thu?		2	te zo?		2	est-ce que tu es?	
3	a bheil e?		3	eñ/hennezh zo?		3	est-ce qu'il est?	
3	a bheil i?		3	hi/hounnezh zo?		3	est-ce qu'elle est?	
1x	a bheil sinn?		1x	ni zo?		1x	est-ce que nous sommes?	
2x	a bheil sibh?		2x	c'hwi zo?		2x	est-ce que vous êtes?	
3x	a bheil iad?		3x	int zo/ar re-se zo?		3x	est-ce qu'ils/elles sont?	

	gaelic			breton	[1]		[2]			français	
3	<u>tha</u>	<u>chan eil</u>	3	<u>ya</u>	<u>n'eo</u> <u>ket</u>	<u>n'emañ</u>	<u>ket</u>	3	<u>oui</u>	<u>non</u>	
1	tha	chan eil	1	ya	n'on ket	n'emaon	ket	1	oui	non	
2	tha	chan eil	2	ya	n'out ket	n'emaout	ket	2	oui	non	
3	tha	chan eil	3	ya	n'eo ket	n'emañ	ket	3	oui	non	
3	tha	chan eil	3	ya	n'eo ket	n'emañ	ket	3	oui	non	
1x	tha	chan eil	1x	ya	n'omp ket	n'emaomp	ket	1x	oui	non	
2x	tha	chan eil	2x	ya	n'oc'h ket	n'emaoc'h	ket	2x	oui	non	
3x	tha	chan eil	3x	ya	n'int ket	n'emaint	ket	3x	oui	non	

[1] *for describing/pour décrire*
[2] *for situating/pour situer*

🏴󠁧󠁢󠁥󠁮󠁧󠁿 english			🐉 welsh cymraeg gallois			🍺 irish gaeilge irlandais		
FUTURE QUESTION								
3	<u>will X</u>	<u>be?</u>	3	<u>fydd X?</u>		3	<u>an mbeidh X?</u>	
1	will I	be?	1	fydda i?		1	an mbeidh mé?	
2	will you	be?	2	fyddi di?		2	an mbeidh tú?	
3	will he	be?	3	fydd e?		3	an mbeidh sé?	
3	will she	be?	3	fydd hi?		3	an mbeidh sí?	
1x	will we	be?	1x	fyddwn ni?		1x	an mbeidh muid?	
2x	will you	be?	2x	fyddwch chi?		2x	an mbeidh sibh?	
3x	will they	be?	3x	fyddan nhw?		3x	an mbeidh siad?	
3	<u>yes</u>	<u>no</u>	3	<u>bydd</u>	<u>na fydd</u> (na)	3	<u>beidh</u>	<u>ní bheidh</u>*
1	yes	no	1	byddaf	na fyddaf (na)	1	beidh	ní bheidh
2	yes	no	2	byddi	na fyddi (na)	2	beidh	ní bheidh
3	yes	no	3	bydd	na fydd (na)	3	beidh	ní bheidh
3	yes	no	3	bydd	na fydd (na)	3	beidh	ní bheidh
1x	yes	no	1x	byddwn	na fyddwn (na)	1x	beidh	ní bheidh
2x	yes	no	2x	byddwch	na fyddwch (na)	2x	beidh	ní bheidh
3x	yes	no	3x	byddan	na fyddan (na)	3x	beidh	ní bheidh

* =cha bheidh (Ulster)

gaelic **gàidhlig** gaélique		breton **brezhoneg** breton			français

FUTUR QUESTION

	gàidhlig		breton			français
3	<u>am bi X?</u>	3	<u>X vo?</u>		3	<u>est-ce qu' X sera?</u>
1	am bi mi?	1	me vo?		1	est-ce que je serai?
2	am bi thu?	2	te vo?		2	est-ce que tu seras?
3	am bi e?	3	eñ/hennezh vo?		3	est-ce qu'il sera?
3	am bi i?	3	hi/hounnezh vo?		3	est-ce qu'elle sera?
1x	am bi sinn?	1x	ni vo?		1x	est-ce que nous serons?
2x	am bi sibh?	2x	c'hwi vo?		2x	est-ce vous serez?
3x	am bi iad?	3x	int vo/ar re-se vo?		3x	est-ce qu'ils/elles seront?

3	<u>bidh</u>	<u>cha bhi</u>	3	<u>ya</u>	<u>X ne vo</u>	<u>ket</u>	3	<u>oui</u>	<u>non</u>
1	bidh	cha bhi	1	ya	ne vin	ket	1	oui	non
2	bidh	cha bhi	2	ya	ne vi	ket	2	oui	non
3	bidh	cha bhi	3	ya	ne vo	ket	3	oui	non
3	bidh	cha bhi	3	ya	ne vo	ket	3	oui	non
1x	bidh	cha bhi	1x	ya	ne vimp	ket	1x	oui	non
2x	bidh	cha bhi	2x	ya	ne viot	ket	2x	oui	non
3x	bidh	cha bhi	3x	ya	ne vint	ket	3x	oui	non

possession

meddu [ar]

seilbh

seilbh

perc'hentiezh

posséder

 english	welsh cymraeg gallois	irish gaeilge irlandais

Statement – Present

	english			welsh	irish
1	I	have	X.	1 mae X gyda fi.	1 tá X agam.
2	you	have	X.	2 mae X gyda ti.	2 tá X agat.
3	he	has	X.	3 mae X gyda fe.	3 tá X aige.
3	she	has	X.	3 mae X gyda hi.	3 tá X aici.
1x	we	have	X.	1x mae X gyda ni.	1x tá X againn.
2x	you	have	X.	2x mae X gyda chi.	2x tá X agaibh.
3x	they	have	X.	3x mae X gyda nhw.	3x tá X acu.

				1	2	
1	I	do	not have X.	dyw X ddim gyda fi.	does dim X gyda fi.	1 níl X agam.*
2	you	do	not have X.	dyw X ddim gyda ti.	does dim X gyda ti.	2 níl X agat.
3	he	does	not have X.	dyw X ddim gyda fe.	does dim X gyda fe.	3 níl X aige.
3	she	does	not have X.	dyw X ddim gyda hi.	does dim X gyda hi.	3 níl X aici.
1x	we	do	not have X.	dyw X ddim gyda ni.	does dim X gyda ni.	1x níl X againn.
2x	you	do	not have X.	dyw X ddim gyda chi.	does dim X gyda chi.	2x níl X agaibh.
3x	they	do	not have X.	dyw X ddim gyda nhw.	does dim X gyda nhw.	3x níl X acu.

[1] *specific/déterminé*
[2] *non-specific/non-déterminé*

* = *chan fhuil X agam (Ulster)*

gaelic gàidhlig gaélique	breton brezhoneg breton	français
		Déclaration – Présent
1 tha X agam.	1 X am eus.	1 j'ai X.
2 tha X agad.	2 X ac'h eus.	2 tu as X.
3 tha X aige.	3 X en deus.	3 il a X.
3 tha X aice.	3 X he deus.	3 elle a X.
1x tha X againn.	1x X hon eus.	1x nous avons X.
2x tha X agaibh.	2x X hoc'h eus.	2x vous avez X.
3x tha X aca.	3x X o deus.	3x ils ont X.

	breton 1	breton 2	français 1	français 2
1 chan eil X agam.	n'em eus ket X	n'em eus ket a* X	je n'ai pas X.	je n'ai pas d'X.
2 chan eil X agad.	n'ec'h eus ket X	n'ec'h eus ket a* X	tu n'as pas X.	tu n'as pas d'X.
3 chan eil X aige.	n'en deus ket X	n'en deus ket a* X	il n'a pas X.	il n'a pas d'X.
3 chan eil X aice.	n'he deus ket X	n'he deus ket a* X	elle n'a pas X.	elle n'a pas d'X.
1x chan eil X againn.	n'hon eus ket X	n'hon eus ket a* X	nous n'avons pas X.	nous n'avons pas d'X.
2x chan eil X agaibh.	n'hoc'h eus ket X	n'hoc'h eus ket a* X	vous n'avez pas X.	vous n'avez pas d'X.
3x chan eil X aca.	n'o deus ket X	n' o deus ket a* X	ils n'ont pas X.	ils n'ont pas d'X.

¹ *specific/déterminé*
² *non-specific/non-déterminé*

¹ *specific/déterminé*
² *non-specific/non-déterminé*

* *'a' is followed by soft mutation*
* *'a' est suivir par la mutation duce*

🇫🇮 english	🐉 welsh cymraeg gallois	🍺 irish gaeilge irlandais

Statement – Future

1	I	will	have X.	1	bydd X gyda fi.
2	you	will	have X.	2	bydd X gyda ti.
3	he	will	have X.	3	bydd X gyda fe.
3	she	will	have X.	3	bydd X gyda hi.
1x	we	will	have X.	1x	bydd X gyda ni.
2x	you	will	have X.	2x	bydd X gyda chi.
3x	they	will	have X.	3x	bydd X gyda nhw.

Irish:
1 beidh X agam.
2 beidh X agat.
3 beidh X aige.
3 beidh X aici.
1x beidh X againn.
2x beidh X agaibh.
3x beidh X acu.

				1	2
1	I	will	not have X.	fydd X ddim gyda fi.	fydd dim X gyda fi.
2	you	will	not have X.	fydd X ddim gyda ti.	fydd dim X gyda ti.
3	he	will	not have X.	fydd X ddim gyda fe.	fydd dim X gyda fe.
3	she	will	not have X.	fydd X ddim gyda hi.	fydd dim X gyda hi.
1x	we	will	not have X.	fydd X ddim gyda ni.	fydd dim X gyda ni.
2x	you	will	not have X.	fydd X ddim gyda chi.	fydd dim X gyda chi.
3x	they	will	not have X.	fydd X ddim gyda nhw.	fydd dim X gyda nhw.

Irish:
1 ní bheidh X agam.*
2 ní bheidh X agat.
3 ní bheidh X aige.
3 ní bheidh X aici.
1x ní bheidh X againn.
2x ní bheidh X agaibh.
3x ní bheidh X acu.

1 *specific/déterminé*
2 *non-specific/non-déterminé*

* =cha bheidh X agam (Ulster)

178

gaelic gàidhlig gaélique	breton brezhoneg breton	français
		Déclaration – Futur

gàidhlig	brezhoneg	français
1 bidh X agam.	1 X am bo.	1 j'aurai X.
2 bidh X agad.	2 X az po.	2 tu auras X.
3 bidh X aige.	3 X en devo.	3 il aura X.
3 bidh X aice.	3 X he devo.	3 elle aura X.
1x bidh X againn.	1x X hor bo.	1x nous aurons X.
2x bidh X agaibh.	2x X ho po.	2x vous aurez X.
3x bidh X aca.	3x X o devo.	3x ils auront X.

gàidhlig	brezhoneg 1	brezhoneg 2	français 1	français 2
1 cha bhi X agam.	N'em bo ket X	N'em bo ket a* X	je n'aurai pas X.	je n'aurai pas d'X.
2 cha bhi X agad.	N'ez po ket X	N'ez po ket a* X	tu n'auras pas X.	tu n'auras pas d'X.
3 cha bhi X aige.	N'en devo ket X	N'en devo ket a* X	il n'aura pas X.	il n'aura pas d'X.
3 cha bhi X aice.	N'he devo ket X	N'he devo ket a* X	elle n'aura pas X.	elle n'aura pas d'X.
1x cha bhi X againn.	N'hor bo ket X	N'hor bo ket a* X	nous n'aurons pas X.	nous n'aurons pas d'X.
2x cha bhi X agaibh.	N'ho po ket X	N'ho po ket a* X	vous n'aurez pas X.	vous n'aurez pas d'X.
3x cha bhi X aca.	N'o devo ket X	N'o devo ket a* X	ils n'auront pas X.	ils n'auront pas d'X.

¹ *specific/déterminé*
² *non-specific/non-déterminé*

*'a' is followed by soft mutation
*'a' est suivir par la mutation duce

¹ *specific/déterminé*
² *non-specific/non-déterminé*

english 	welsh cymraeg gallois	irish gaeilge irlandais

Question – Present

specific/déterminé:

1	do	I	have X?	yes	no
2	do	you	have X?	yes	no
3	does	he	have X?	yes	no
3	does	she	have X?	yes	no
1x	do	we	have X?	yes	no
2x	do	you	have X?	yes	no
3x	do	they	have X?	yes	no

1	ydi X gyda fi?	ydi	nac ydi/nac yw (na)
2	ydi X gyda ti?	ydi	nac ydi/nac yw (na)
3	ydi X gyda fe?	ydi	nac ydi/nac yw (na)
3	ydi X gyda hi?	ydi	nac ydi/nac yw (na)
1x	ydi X gyda ni?	ydi	nac ydi/nac yw (na)
2x	ydi X gyda chi?	ydi	nac ydi/nac yw (na)
3x	ydi X gyda nhw?	ydi	nac ydi/nac yw (na)

non-specific/non-déterminé:

1	oes X gyda fi?	oes	nac oes (na)
2	oes X gyda ti?	oes	nac oes (na)
3	oes X gyda fe?	oes	nac oes (na)
3	oes X gyda hi?	oes	nac oes (na)
1x	oes X gyda ni?	oes	nac oes (na)
2x	oes X gyda chi?	oes	nac oes (na)
3x	oes X gyda nhw?	oes	nac oes (na)

1	an bhfuil X agam?	tá	níl*
2	an bhfuil X agat?	tá	níl
3	an bhfuil X aige?	tá	níl
3	an bhfuil X aici?	tá	níl
1x	an bhfuil X againn?	tá	níl
2x	an bhfuil X agaibh?	tá	níl
3x	an bhfuil X acu?	tá	níl

* = *chan fhuil (Ulster)*

Déclaration – Présent

gàidhlig			brezhoneg		français		
1	a bheil X agam?	tha chan eil	1 X am eus?	ya n'em eus ket	1 est-ce que j'ai X?	oui non
2	a bheil X agad?	tha chan eil	2 X ac'h eus?	ya n'ec'h eus ket	2 est-ce que tu as X?	oui non
3	a bheil X aige?	tha chan eil	3 X en deus?	ya n'en deus ket	3 est-ce qu'il a X?	oui non
3	a bheil X aice?	tha chan eil	3 X he deus?	ya n'he deus ket	3 est-ce qu'elle a X?	oui non
1x	a bheil X againn?	tha chan eil	1x X hon eus?	ya n'hon eus ket	1x est-ce que nous avons X?	oui non
2x	a bheil X agaibh?	tha chan eil	2x X hoc'h eus?	ya n'hoc'h eus ket	2x est-ce que vous avez X?	oui non
3x	a bheil X aca?	tha chan eil	3x X o deus?	ya n'o deus ket	3x est-ce qu'ils ont X?	oui non

 english

 welsh cymraeg gallois

 irish gaeilge irlandais

Question – Future

english	welsh cymraeg gallois	irish gaeilge irlandais
1 will I have X? yes no	1 fydd X gyda fi? bydd na fydd (na)	1 an mbeidh X agam? beidh ní bheidh*
2 will you have X? yes no	2 fydd X gyda ti? bydd na fydd (na)	2 an mbeidh X agat? beidh ní bheidh
3 will he have X? yes no	3 fydd X gyda fe? bydd na fydd (na)	3 an mbeidh X aige? beidh ní bheidh
3 will she have X? yes no	3 fydd X gyda hi? bydd na fydd (na)	3 an mbeidh X aici? beidh ní bheidh
1x will we have X? yes no	1x fydd X gyda ni? bydd na fydd (na)	1x an mbeidh X againn? beidh ní bheidh
2x will you have X? yes no	2x fydd X gyda chi? bydd na fydd (na)	2x an mbeidh X agaibh? beidh ní bheidh
3x will they have X? yes no	3x fydd X gyda nhw? bydd na fydd (na)	3x an mbeidh X acu? beidh ní bheidh

* = cha bheidh (Ulster)

gaelic
gàidhlig gaélique

breton
brezhoneg breton

français

	gaelic				breton				français		

Question – Futur

1	am bi X agam?	bidh	cha bhi	1	X vo ganin?	ya	ne vo ket	**1**	est-ce que j'aurai X?	oui	non
2	am bi X agad?	bidh	cha bhi	2	X vo ganez?	ya	ne vo ket	**2**	est-ce que tu auras X?	oui	non
3	am bi X aige?	bidh	cha bhi	3	X vo gantañ?	ya	ne vo ket	**3**	est-ce qu'il aura X?	oui	non
3	am bi X aice?	bidh	cha bhi	3	X vo ganti?	ya	ne vo ket	**3**	est-ce qu'elle aura X?	oui	non
1x	am bi X againn?	bidh	cha bhi	1x	X vo ganeomp?	ya	ne vo ket	**1x**	est-ce que nous aurons X?	oui	non
2x	am bi X agaibh?	bidh	cha bhi	2x	X vo ganeoc'h?	ya	ne vo ket	**2x**	est-ce que vous aurez X?	oui	non
3x	am bi X aca?	bidh	cha bhi	3x	X vo ganto?	ya	ne vo ket	**3x**	est-ce qu'ils auront X?	oui	non

3x ils=masculine plural
or mixed/elles=feminine plural

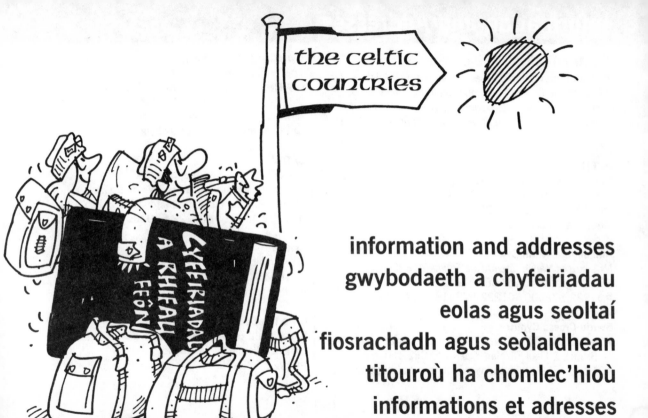

information and addresses
gwybodaeth a chyfeiriadau
eolas agus seoltaí
fiosrachadh agus seòlaidhean
titouroù ha chomlec'hioù
informations et adresses

Cymru Wales Pays de Galles

Dial your international access code (e.g. 00) followed by
44, then the telephone number omitting the initial 0.
*Composez le code international (par exemple 00) et le
numéro 44, et après le numéro de téléphone sans le 0.*

ACEN
Welsh Language Services/*Services de la langue galloise*
1 Stryd y Bont, Caerdydd CF1 2TH
☎01222 665455 📠01222 668810 📧data@acen.co.uk
🖥http://www.acen.co.uk

Amgueddfa Werin Cymru
Museum of Welsh Life/*Musée Folklorique Galloise*
Sain Ffagan, Caerdydd CF5 6XB
☎01222 573500 📠01222 578413

Bwrdd Croeso Cymru
Wales Tourist Board/*Conseil de Tourisme du Pays de Galles*
Tŷ Brunel, 2 Heol Fitzalan, Caerdydd CF2 1UY
☎01222 499909 🖥http://www.tourism.wales.gov.uk

Bwrdd yr Iaith Gymraeg
The Welsh Language Board/*Conseil de la langue galloise*
5-7 Heol Eglwys Fair, Caerdydd CF1 2AT
☎01222 224744 📠01222 224577
📧bwrdd_yr_iaith@netwales.co.uk
🖥http://www.netwales.co.uk/byig

CADW
Welsh Historic Monuments
Monuments Historiques du Pays de Galles
Tŷ Brunel, Heol Fitzalan, Caerdydd CF2 1UY
☎01222 465511 📠01222 500200

Celtica
Machynlleth, Powys SY20 8ER
☎01654 702702 📠01654 703604
🖥 http://www.celtica.wales.com

Clwb Ifor Bach
Welsh night club in Cardiff/*Boîte de nuit galloise*
11 Heol Womanby, Caerdydd
☎01222 232199

Cymdeithas Cymru-Llydaw
Wales-Brittany Society/*Association Galles-Bretagne*
Guto Rhys, 36 Heol Clive, Treganna, Caerdydd CF5 1HJ
☎01222 223262

Cymdeithas yr Iaith Gymraeg
Welsh Language Society/*Association du gallois*
15 Rhodfa'r Gogledd, Aberystwyth SY23 2JH
☎01970 624501 ▤01970 627122
✉swyddfa@cymdeithas.com
▭http://www.cymdeithas.com

Cymru a'r Byd
Wales International/*Pays de Galles Internationale*
Muriau Gwyn, Beulah, Castell Newydd Emlyn SA38 9QE
☎01239 810752 ▤01239 811655

Eisteddfod Genedlaethol Cymru
Welsh National Eisteddfod
40 Parc Tŷ Glas, Llanisien, Caerdydd CF4 5WU
☎01222 763777 ▤01222 237071
▭http://www.eisteddfod.org.uk

Youth Hostel Association of England and Wales
Trevelyan House, St. Stephen's Hill, St. Albans Herts,
AL1 2DY. England/Angleterre ☎ 01727 855215

Youth Hostels Association
Association des Auberges de Jeunesse
1 Heol y Gadeirlan, Caerdydd CF1 9HA ☎01222 396766

International Youth Hostel Federation
Fédération des Auberges de Jeunesse
9 Guessens Road, Welwyn Garden City, Hartfordshire
AL8 6QW, England/Angleterre
☎01707 332487 ▤01707 323980

Éire Ireland Irlande

Dial your international access code (e.g. 00) followed by 353 (44 for the North), then the telephone number omitting the initial 0.

Composez le code international (par exemple 00) et le numéro 353 (44 pour le Nord), et après le numéro de téléphone sans le 0.

Áis
Irish Language Books Council
31 Stáid na bhFininí, Baile Átha Cliath 2

Bord na Gaeilge
Irish Language Board/*Conseil de la langue irlandaise*
7 Cearnóg Mhuirfean, Baile Átha Cliath 2
☎01 676 3222 📠01 661 6564 ✉bng@iol.ie
🖳http://www.atlanticisland.ie/atlanticisland/bng/

Comhdháil Náisiúnta na Gaeilge
46 Sráid Chill Dara, Baile Átha Cliath 2
☎01 679 4780 📠01 679 0214

An Roinn Ealaíon, Cultúir agus Gaeltachta
Ministry for Arts, Culture and Gaeltacht
Dún Aimhirgín, Bóthar Mespil, Baile Átha Cliath 4
☎01 667 0788 GTN 7111 📠01 667 0826

An Bord Fáilte
Irish Tourist Board/*Conseil de Tourisme de l'Irlande*
Baggot Street Bridge, Baile Átha Cliath 2
☎01 602 4000 📠01 602 4100
🖳http://www.ireland.travel.ie

The Northern Ireland Tourist Board
Conseil de Tourisme de l'Irlande du Nord
Tourist Information Centre, St. Ann's Court,
59 North Street, Béal Feirste/Belfast BT1 1NB
☎01232 246609 📠01232 240960
🖳http://www.ni-tourism.com

Alba Scotland Ecosse

Dial your international access code (e.g. 00) followed by 44, then the telephone number ommitting the initial 0.
Composez le code international (par exemple 00) et le numéro 44, et après le numéro de téléphone sans le 0.

Acair
Gaelic Publishers
7 Sraid Sheumais, Steòrnabhagh, Leòdhas HS1 2QN
☎01851 703020 🖷01851 703294 ✉acair@sol.org.uk

An Comunn Gàidhealach
The Gaelic Society/*l'Association Gaélique*
109 Sràid na h-Eaglaise, Inbhir Nis IV1 1EY
☎01463 231226 🖷01463 715557
🖥 http://www.glen.co.uk/mod/an_comun.html

Comann an Luchd-Ionnsachaidh
Gaelic Learners' Society
Association des débutants en gaélique
3 High Street, Inbhir Pheofharain, Siorramachd Rois
IV15 9HL ☎🖷01349 862820
🖥http://www.smo.uhi.ac.uk/gaidhlig/buidhnean/cli

Comhairle nan Leabhraichean
Gaelic Books Council
22 Sràid Achadh a' Mhansa, Glaschu G11 5QP
☎0141 337 6211 🖷0141 341 0515
✉fios@gaelicbooks.demon.co.uk
🖥http://www.gaelicbooks.org.uk

Comunn na Gàidhlig
Gaelic Society/Association du gaélique
Tourist information to Gaelic Scotland/*Info. touristique sur l'Écosse gaélique*
5 Caolshràid Mhìcheil, Inbhir Nis IV2 3HQ
☎01463 711792 🖥http://www.smo.uhi.ac.uk/cnag/
✉fios@cnag.org.uk

Dalriada Celtic Heritage Trust
Dun na Beatha, 2 Brathwic Place, Brodick, Isle of Arran, KA27 8BN
☎🖷01770 302049
🖥http://www.dalriada.co.uk ✉dalriada@dalriada.co.uk

Lèirsinn
Gaelic Affairs Research Centre
Centre de recherches des affaires gaéliques
Sabhal Mòr Ostaig, An Teanga, Slèite, An t-Eilean
Sgiathanach, IV44 8RQ
☎01471 844288 📠01471 844368
🖥http://www.smo.uhi.ac.uk/smo/leirsinn.html
✉leirsinn@smo.uhi.ac.uk

Sabhal Mòr Ostaig
Gaelic college/Collège gaélique
An Teanga, Slèite, An t-Eilean Sgiathanach IV44 8RQ
☎01471 844373 📠01471 844383
🖥http://www.smo.uhi.ac.uk

Scottish Tourist Board
Conseil de Tourisme de l'Écosse
Central Information Department, PO Box 705,
Dùn Èideann/Edinburgh EH4 3EU
☎0131 332 2433 📠0131 315 4545
🖥http://www.holiday.scotland.net

Breizh Brittany Bretagne

Dial your international access code (e.g. 00) followed by 33, then the telephone number omitting the initial 0.
Composez le code international (par exemple 00) et le numéro 33, et après le numéro de téléphone sans le 0.

Servij ar Brezhoneg
Breton Language Services/*Service de la Langue Bretonne*
Skol Uhel ar Vro/Institut Culturel de Bretagne
1 rue Raoul Ponchon, 35069 ROAZHON/RENNES Cédex
☎02.99.87.58.00 🖷02.99.38.50.32

Skol-Veur Hañv Breizh / Université d'Été de Bretagne
Breton courses/*Cours de breton*
5 straed Pasteur, 56100 AN ORIANT/LORIENT
☎02.97.64.19.90 🖷02.97.64.20.45

Roudour
Breton courses/*Cours de breton*
Bp 24 - Hent Berrien, 29690 AN HUELGOAD/HUELGOAT
☎02.98.99.75.81 🖷02.98.99.76.01

Stur-Strollad Urzhiataerezh/Kevredigezh 1901
Breton computer group/*Groupe informatique breton*
6 Straed Lapique, 22000 SANT-BRIEG/SAINT BRIEUC
☎02.96.94.44.56

Mirdi An Tiegez Gwechall
Museum of old-style houses/*La Maison de nos Ancêtres*
22 Hent Lanniliz, 29880 PLOUGERNE/PLOUGUER
☎02.98.04.72.44

Park an Arvorig/Parc d'Armorique
BP 35, Menez Meur, 29460 HANVEG ☎02.98.21.90.69

Maison des Gîtes de France
Ask for/demandez "Chambres d'Hôtes en Bretagne"
59 rue Saint Lazare, 75009 PARIS, France
☎01.49.70.75.75 🖷01.42.81.28.53
Minitel: 36.15 GITES DE FRANCE

Comité Régional du Tourisme de Bretagne
74 bis rue de Paris, 35069 RENNES
☎02.99.28.44.30 🖷02.99.28.44.40

Maison de la Bretagne/Formules Bretagne
17 rue de l'Arrivée, 75737 PARIS CÉDEX 15
France ☎01.42.79.07.07

Service de Réservation Gîtes de France Côtes d'Armor/ Aodoù an Arvor
21-23 rue des Promenades - BP 4536
22045 SAINT-BRIEUC/SANT BRIEG CÉDEX 2
☎02.96.62.21.73 📠02.96.61.20.16

Service de Réservation Gîtes de France Finistère/Penn ar Bed
5 allée Sully, 29322 QUIMPER/KEMPER CÉDEX 2
☎02.98.52.48.00 📠02.98.52.48.44

Service de Réservation Gîtes de France Ille et Vilaine/Il ha Gwilun
Loisirs Accueil - 8 rue de Coëtquen
BP 5093 - 35061 RENNES/ROAZHON CÉDEX 3
☎02.99.78.47.57 📠02.99.78.47.53

Service de Réservation Gîtes de France Loire-Atlantique/Liger-Atlantel
1 allée Baco, NANTES/NAONED
☎02.51.72.95.65 📠02.40.35.17.05

Service de Réservation Gîtes de France Morbihan
2 rue du Château - BP 318 - 56403 AURAY
☎02.97.56.48.12 📠02.97.50.70.07

CASINO - Cafétéria Service Groupes
Ask for a map of their cafeterias – very good value
Demandez la carte des cafétérias – bon marché
24, rue de la montat, 42008 Saint-Étienne Cédex 2
France ☎04.77.45.44.01 📠04.77.45.48.50

- Another good restaurant/cafeteria is **Flunch**
  *Un autre restaurant/cafétéria est **Flunch***
- **Formula 1** offers cheap hotel accommodation in France
  *Il y a des hôtels **Formula 1** en France à bon prix*

Other Addresses D'autres Adresses

The European Bureau for Lesser Used Languages
Sint-Jooststraat/rue Saint-Josse 49, B-1210
Bruxelles/Brussel, Belgium/Belgique
☎+32 (0)2 218.25.90 📄+32 (0)2 218.19.74
✉pub00341@innet.be 🖥http://www.eblul-bic.be

Mercator
Prifysgol Cymru, Llanbadarn, Aberystwyth,
SY23 3AS, Wales
✉merc@aber.ac.uk
🖥http://www.aber.ac.uk/~merwww/

the media
y cyfryngau
na meáin chumarsáide
na meadhanan
ar media
le média

Cymru Wales *Pays de Galles*

BBC Radio Cymru 92-105 FM
National Welsh language radio/Radio nationale en gallois

Radio Ceredigion – 96.6 & 103.3 FM
Local Welsh language radio/Radio locale en gallois

Radio Sain Abertawe – 1170 AM
Welsh language radio in the south/Radio en gallois au sud

S4C
Welsh Channel 4 TV/Chaîne 4 galloise
Parc Tŷ Glas, Llanisien, Caerdydd CF4 5DU
⌨ http://www.s4c.co.uk
The evening news is available through the internet:
⌨ http://www.bbc.co.uk/news/ (click on the 'newyddion' button)

Y Cymro
Parc Busnes, Ffordd Wrecsam, Yr Wyddgrug
CH7 1XY ☎01352 700022 📠01352 752180
⌨ http://www.nwn.co.uk

Golwg
Blwch Post 4, Llanbedr Pont Steffan SA48 7LX
☎01570 423529 📠01570 423538

Éire Ireland *Irlande*

Radio na Life 102.2 FM
Irish language radio in Dublin/Radio en irlandais à Dublin
☎01 661 6333

Raidió na Gaeltachta 92.6-102.7 FM
Limited service available on satellite – Astra 1b in Europe
and Galaxy 5 in North America. Daily news in Irish
available through the internet.
☎091 506677 📠091 506666 ✉rng@rte.ie
⌨http://www.rte.ie/radio/rnag/

Teilifís na Gaeilge (TnaG)
Irish TV channel/chaine de télé en irlandais
☎01 667 0944 📠01 667 0946 ⌨http://www.tnag.ie

Radio Telefís Éireann (RTÉ)
Donnybrook, Baile Átha Cliath 4
☎01 208 3111 📠01 208 6080 ⌨http://www.rte.ie

Anois
27 Cearnóg Mhuirfean, Baile Átha Cliath 2
☎01 676 0268

Alba Scotland *Ecosse*

Cothrom
Internet Edition ✉northwest@cali.co.uk

BBC Radio nan Gaidheal 103.5-105 FM
Broadcasts an average of 45 hours each week
Queen Margaret Drive, Glaschu G12 8DG
⌨http://www.smo.uhi.ac.uk/bbcalba

Camataidh Craolaidh Gàidhlig
Gaelic Broadcasting Committee
4 Acarsaid, Cidhe Shràid Chrombail, Steòrnabhagh,
Eilean Leodhais HS1 2DF
☎01851 705550 📄706432 ✉comataidh@compuserve.com

Cothrom
Magazine for learners/Revue pour débutants en gaélique
Comann an Luchd-Ionnsachaidh, 62 Prìomhshràid,
Inbhir Ghòrdain, Siooachd Rois, IV18 0DH
✉cli@gaelic.net

Guth na Gàidhlig
Highland News Group, Henderson Road, Inbhir Nis
IV1 1SP

The Scotsman
An Drochaid a Tuath, Dùn Èideann/Edinburgh EH1 1YT
☎0131 650 3624 📄0131 243 3686
⌨http://www.scotsman.com

The West Highland Free Press
An t-Ath Leathann, An t-Eilean Sgitheanach
☎01471 822464 📄01471 822691
✉newsdesk@whfp.co.uk

The Stornoway Gazette
10 Sràid Fhrangain, Steòrnabhagh, Eilean Leodhais
HS1 2XE ⌨http://www.hebrides.com

Breizh Brittany *Bretagne*

Radio Kreiz Breizh 102.9 FM & 106.5 FM
Breton Radio in Central Brittany
Radio Bretne en Centre Bretagne

France 3
News in Breton/*Nouvelles en breton*
⌨http://www.france3.fr ✉tvtel3@france3.fr

Bremañ
Skol an Emsav, 8 straed Hoche, Roazhon

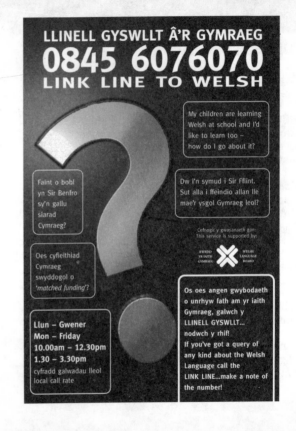

WELCOME TO FINISTÈRE!
DEGEMER MAD E PENN AR BED!

The best way to explore Finistère from the coast to the rural heartland, is to place yourself in the hands of those who live there …

- **CHOICE:** Gîtes de France in Finistère offer: 1 150 self catering gîtes, 360 rooms offering Bed and Breakfast and 15 countryside campsites

- **QUALITY:** All of our properties are regularly checked and classified according to a system of «Epis» (ears of corn), indicating the degree of comfort and standard of equipment provided in the accommodation on a scale from 1 to 3.

- **VALUE FOR MONEY:** For example: Gîte, 3 ears of corn, 4/5pers, 3 Km from sandy beaches, 1 week in June : 1 400 FF

Gîtes de France in Finistère: Brittany at its best!

If you want further information and/or order one of our publications, please send the booking form to: GÎTES DE FRANCE FINISTÈRE - 5 Allée Sully - 29322 QUIMPER Cedex - France (☎ 00.33.2.98.52.48.00 Fax: 00.33.2.98.52.48.44 E-Mail : gites29@eurobretagne.fr)

Full name: _____ **Address:** _____

Tel: _____ **Fax:** _____ **E-Mail:** _____

Please send me the following guide(s) and/or CD-Rom:

Self-catering – Finistère (1 150 gîtes) - (French version + English translations) Guide ____ x 70 FF = ____ FF

Self-catering – Finistère (621 gîtes) (French-English) - CD-Rom ____ x 70 FF = ____ FF

SPECIAL OFFER: GUIDE + CD-Rom for 99 FF only ____ x 99 FF = ____ FF

Typical Breton Gîtes – Finistère (15 gîtes) (French - English) FREE

Bed and Breakfast – Brittany (1 500 rooms) (French version only) ____ x 20 FF = ____ FF

Countryside campsites – Brittany (36 campsites) (French-English) FREE

I enclose a cheque for _____ FF as payment

books about Wales
and the Celtic nations

Art

JAMES BOGLE
Artists in Snowdonia
£5.95   0 86243 222 7

RON DAVIES
Images of Wales
£3.95 hardback   0 86243 226 X

MARIAN DELYTH (ED.)
Cymru'r Camera
(Photographer's Wales)
£4.95 hardback   0 86243 031 3

NICHOLAS EVANS AND RHODA EVANS
Delwau Duon *(Symphonies in Black)*
£9.95 hardback   0 86243 135 2

ANTHONY GRIFFITHS
Snowdonia – Myth and Image
£5.95   0 86243 276 6

HYWEL HARRIES
Cymru'r Cynfas *(Wales on Canvas)*
£9.50   0 86243 356 8

Children

MANON EAMES, IOAN HEFIN & MARY PRICE JENKINS
The House That Jack Built
£4.95 hardback   0 86243 313 4

RHIANNON IFANS
Tales from Wales
£3.95   0 86243 182 4

RHIANNON IFANS
The Legends of King Arthur
£3.95 hardback   0 86243 210 3

RHIANNON IFANS
The Magic of the Mabinogion
£4.95   0 86243 174 3

Cookery

BOBBY FREEMAN
First Catch Your Peacock
£9.95   0 86243 315 0

BOBBY FREEMAN
Welsh Country Cookery
£2.95   0 86243 133 6

BOBBY FREEMAN
Welsh Recipe Booklets
1. A Book of Welsh Bread
£1.45   0 86243 137 9
2. A Book of Welsh Country Cakes and Buns
£1.45   0 86243 138 7
3. A Book of Welsh Bakestone Cookery
£1.45   0 86243 139 5
4. A Book of Welsh Country Puddings and Pies
£1.45   0 86243 140 9
5. A Book of Welsh Fish Cookery
£1.45   0 86243 141 7
6. A Book of Welsh Soups and Savouries
£1.45   0 86243 142 5

DAVE FROST
Welsh Salad Days
£8.95   0 86243 383 5

DUDLE NEWBERY
Dudley: Welsh TV Chef
£8.95   0 86243 439 4

CHRISTINE SMEETH
The Welsh Table
£5.95   0 86243 305 3

HELEN SMITH-TWIDDY
Celtic Cookbook
£2.95   0 904864 50 2

Language Tutors

HEINI GRUFFUDD
It's Welsh!
£4.95   0 86243 245 6

also:
It's Welsh! – cassette
£4.95   0 86243 297 9

HEINI GRUFFUDD
Get By in Welsh
£1.95   0 86243 181 6

HEINI GRUFFUDD
Welcome to Welsh
£4.95   0 86243 069 0

also:
Welcome to Welsh – cassette
£4.95   0 86243 298 7

HEINI GRUFFUDD & ELWYN IOAN
Welsh is Fun!
£2.95   0 9500178 4 1

HEINI GRUFFUDD & ELWYN IOAN
Welsh is Fun-tastic!
£2.95   0 9500178 7 6

HEINI GRUFFUDD
The Welsh Learner's Dictionary
£5.95   0 86243 363 0

LEONARD HAYLES
Welsh Phrases for Learners
£5.95   0 86243 364 9

DAN LYNN JAMES
Meithrin y Dysgwyr
£2.95   0 904864 08 1

FLANN O'RIAIN
Lazy Way to Welsh
£4.95   0 86243 240 5

Hwylio 'Mlaen *(Sail On!)*
GLENYS M.ROBERTS (ED.)

DUNCAN BROWN
Gwerth y Byd yn Grwn *(Worth the Whole Wide World)*
£3.95   0 86243 365 7

KATE CROCKETT
Y Sîn Roc *(The Rock Scene)*
£3.95   0 86243 370 3

ELWYN HUGHES
Sgyrsiau Dros Baned *(Chats over a Cuppa)*
£3.95   0 86243 326 6

ELIN MEEK
Sêr Heddiw *(Stars of Today)*
£3.95   0 86243 329 0

ELIN MEEK
Cymry wrth eu Gwaith *(The Welsh at work)*
£3.95   0 86243 393 2

SIÔN MEREDITH
Teithiau Car *(Car Trips)*
£3.95   0 86243 327 4

GLENYS M.ROBERTS
Llyfrau Cymraeg Enwog *(Famous Welsh Books)*
£3.95   0 86243 366 5

CATRIN STEVENS
Cymry Ddoe *(The Welsh of Yesterday)*
£3.95   0 86243 328 2

PHILIP WYN JONES
Ffilmiau Cymreig
£3.95   0 86243 443 2

HEINI GRUFFUDD
Cyfle i Siarad
£3.95   0 86243 444 0

Other Celtic languages

GEORGE JONES
Lazy Way to Gaelic
£5.95   0 86243 308 8

AODÁN MAC PÓILÍN
Irish is Fun!
£3.95   0 86243 143 3

SEAN O'RIAIN
Irish is Fun-tastic!
£3.95   0 86243 207 3

FLANN O'RIAIN
Lazy Way to Irish
£5.95   0 86243 287 1

Related books:
Irish is Fun/Irish is Fun-tastic is available from Ais, 31 Straid na bhfinini, Baile Átha Cliath 2 (Dublin 2), Éire; tel: 00 353 763222

Gaelic is Fun! has also been published and is available from Acair, 7 Sraid Sheumais (James St.), Steornabhagh (Stornoway), Alba; tel: 01851 3020.

Miscellaneous

TINA CARR & ANNEMARIE SCHÖNE
Pigs and Ingots
£9.95   0 86243 286 3

RON DAVIES
The Seven Wonders of Wales
£2.95   0 86243 292 8

DAVID GREENSLADE
Burning Down the Dosbarth
£5.95   0 86243 271 5

HEINI GRUFFUDD
Welsh Names for Children
£3.95   0 904864 99 5

HEINI GRUFFUDD
Wales: The Nation
£5.95   0 86243 423 8

COLIN PALFREY
The Scottish Trip
£1.95   0 86243 041 0

CHRIS THOMAS
The Holiday Angler in Wales
£6.95   0 86243 375 4

CHRIS THOMAS
Friendly Fishing Hotels of Wales
£6.95   0 86243 424 6

Music

STUART BROWN (ED.)
Sosban Fach
£3.95   0 86243 134 4

RYAN DAVIES
Caneuon Ryan (Ryan's Songs)
£4.95   0 86243 061 5